T0331500

Industry 1.0 to 4.0

1. 0. Steam Engine, Steel Production, Textiles

2.0. Production Line, Mass Production

3.0. Computer, Internet, Digital Net

4.0. Autonomous Machines, IoT, Smart Factory, Cyber-Physical

TECHNOLOGY FOR BUSINESS

TECHNOLOGY FOR BUSINESS

Application of the Advances in
Industry 4.0 to Small to Medium Sized Enterprises

John Blakemore

JENNY STANFORD
PUBLISHING

Published by

Jenny Stanford Publishing Pte. Ltd.
101 Thomson Road
#06-01, United Square
Singapore 307591

Email: editorial@jennystanford.com
Web: www.jennystanford.com

British Library Cataloguing-in-Publication Data
A catalogue record for this book is available from the British Library.

Technology for Business: Application of the Advances in Industry 4.0 to Small to Medium Sized Enterprises

Copyright © 2023 Jenny Stanford Publishing Pte. Ltd.

ISBN 978-981-4968-70-6 (Hardcover)
ISBN 978-1-003-38216-4 (eBook)

Contents

Preface

This book is about the new tools of what is commonly called the "Fourth Industrial Revolution" and how predominantly small to medium sized businesses can benefit from them to increase productivity and profitability.

Large businesses are already using either all or most of these methods, but the smaller enterprises can struggle with day-to-day problems and lack of funds to adequately allow for the improvements in business processes that are absolutely necessary.

Whilst the identification and definition of all the latest tools can be readily recognised, the way and where these should be implemented is not so easy.

This book postulates that an organisational framework based on the Lean principles established in the automotive industry in Japan is necessary if the maximum benefit from introducing and using the new tools is to be realised.

Acknowledgements

Special acknowledgements to the following:

1. Dr Ezzelino Leonardi, Technical Director, Pirelli Cables
2. Mr Colin Bale, CEO, Pirelli Cables
3. Dr Chris Roberts, CEO, Cochlear
4. Mr John Quinn, MD, Thorn Lighting
5. Dr Bob Blake, VP, Precision Valves Inc
6. Mr Tim Evans, Director, Moore Business
7. Mr Charles E. Smith, CEO, Moore Business
8. Mr Nick Stump, CEO, Comalco
9. Mr Bruce McGilvray, MD, Rickett and Colman
10. Mr Richard Hammond, CEO, Adelaide Brighton
11. Mr Norris Little, President, Shaw USA
12. Dr Farhad Shafaghi, CEO, Advanced Manufacturing Centre
13. Prof Vernon Ireland, Australian Graduate School of Engineering Innovation
14. Prof Simon Sheather, University of NSW
15. Prof Dexter Dunphy, University of Technology Sydney
16. All the staff at Canon for ongoing support
17. Mr Bill Ferme, Manufacturing Consultant, Ferme Eng
18. Mr Murray Clair, CEO, Nupress

Chapter 1

Introduction

Summary

The four industrial revolutions that took place in 1736, 1870, 1969, and 2004, are briefly described. All of these had elements that immediately impacted on business efficiencies and profitability. When the tools are applied using Lean systems combined with Statistical Process Control, the business may be continuously improved as the opportunity for new innovations become observable as much of the extraneous data is removed and the focus becomes sharper. All functions of in our society in engineering, science, medicine, music, space, mathematics, manufacturing, etc., have already been revolutionised and this will be never ending. We can future proof our business with artificial intelligence and the Internet of Things. We are only limited by our imagination.

This book is primarily about the technological aspects of industry 4.0. It recognises that it is not necessarily possible to pin precise times to each of the so-called revolutions, so the dates for the beginning of each is based on a consensus approach.

The book also recognises that the technological aspects of running a business must be driven and strategized by people, so the human element and how it responds to the changes in technology must remain at the forefront of our mind. Hence to be

Technology for Business: Application of the Advances in Industry 4.0 to Small to Medium Sized Enterprises
John Blakemore
Copyright © 2023 Jenny Stanford Publishing Pte. Ltd.
ISBN 978-981-4968-70-6 (Hardcover), 978-1-003-38216-4 (eBook)
www.jennystanford.com

successful a business must not only adapt to the rapid increase in technologies but the leadership and business culture must be conducive to change. I analysed this in some detail in my book *The Quality Solution*, so it will not be repeated here.

The Internet of Things (IoT) has changed our life in every way. Artificial intelligence (AI) is all around us and now guiding us almost unnoticed. It has been readily accepted as it fused with our way of life. In particular, it has been the precursor to what has been defined as Smart processes and Smart Manufacturing, which use all the elements of our rich imagination. Most of us are familiar with Alexa or Siri. Climate change, the resultant use of renewables, rapid globalisation, are all being fuelled by the tools of what is loosely called the Fourth Industrial Revolution or what is called Industry 4.0. This gradual revolution has been going on for some time and in some cases almost unnoticed. All of us now are familiar with the improved communication afforded to us with the ubiquitous mobile phone. The power of his device expands, exponentially, and it is so important that we can never be without it. The fact that we carry it with us all the time means that we can be in contact almost instantaneously with almost anyone anywhere and access almost all forms of information instantaneously.

The Internet of Things, wide use of sensors, robotics and machine to machine communication, as far as manufacturing is concerned, can lead to the complete replacement of old methods of batch manufacturing with something approaching continuous flow. Smart machines can analyse and diagnose issues without the need for human intervention or at least continuously monitor situations to predict and help prevent catastrophic failure. Virtual Reality (VR) can supply diagnostic and fault fixing methodologies through the glasses to the user for instant understanding and a remedy of problems. The Japanese ideal of total prevention of failure can possibly be achieved. However, the fundamental framework of the business must be in place for any of the elements of industry 4.0 to be of value. These advances in manufacturing are readily transferred into other fields of endeavour.

The phone and the Apps on it provide information at a level and accuracy never seen before. Through Google earth we have access to knowledge of over 200 countries.

A team of German scientists were probably the first to coin the phrase the "Fourth Industrial Revolution".

Klaus Schwab expanded on the concept as follows:

"The possibilities of billions of people connected by mobile devices with unprecedented processing power, storage capacity and access to knowledge, are unlimited. This will be magnified by the emerging technological advances in artificial intelligence, robotics, the Internet of Things, virtual reality, 3-D printing, nanotechnology, biotechnology, materials science, energy storage, and quantum computing."

In summary, the four stages of the Industrial revolution can best be illustrated by the following diagram:

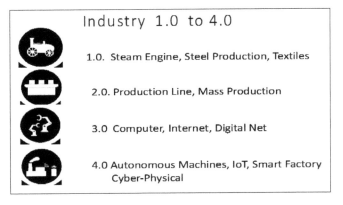

Figure 1.1 Schematic illustration of what is generally recognised as the stages of the Industrial Revolution.

The First Industrial Revolution (1736)

In 1709, in England, Abraham Darby produced pig iron from coke rather than charcoal. In 1712, Thomas Newcomen invented the steam engine. However, it is generally accepted that the First Industrial Revolution began in Scotland and with the inventions of James Watt. The availability of coal was one of coal was one the main drivers. It is ironic that coal, once revered, is now reviled as the major cause of global warming and climate change.

Scottish Engineer James Watt (1736–1819), sent a note to his friend John Robinson as follows:

> "I have now made an engine that shall not waste a particle of steam. It shall be boiling hot."

He had perfected a condenser to add to the steam engine. The acceleration of the Industrial revolution had begun. Prior to this, steam-engine technology had been used, but these machines depended on steam condensing inside a large cylinder after the cylinder was cooled. It was hence relatively inefficient. James Watt's invention changed the whole of the world, and his invention is generally recognised as the beginning of the First Industrial Revolution. Trevithick then built the first engine powered by high pressure.

Figure 1.2 Trevithick engine powered by high pressure steam (1799).

The Second Industrial Revolution (1870)

The invention of electricity and the work particularly of Nicola Tesla, led to mass production lines and in particular the production of products like the model T Ford. Henry Ford and

Thomas Edison also built the first electric car at this time. Its development was curtailed when, despite the fact that Ford and Edison both acknowledged the risks that they would raise the ire of the oil companies, and had taken the precaution to have their own fire engine on standby, there laboratory and prototype plant was burnt to the ground. Deciding that the risks were too great, Ford and Edison abandoned their project and even when a second attempt at the electric car was made by General Motors and Honda in California. These cars were leased to users and then recalled and crushed even though most users wanted to buy them.

Figure 1.3 T Model Ford Flywheel magnetos for the T Model Ford on a moving production conveyor belt at Highland Park Michigan Plant USA. This was the first use of a moving conveyor belt production and assembly.

Mass production techniques for the production of motor cars was still the preferred method until Dr W. E. Deming, a statistician, changed the way we make cars forever by linking the Lean methods of production practised by the Japanese with Statistical process control (SPC). This has now progressed even further using the Japanese Kaizen philosophy of continuous improvement. Dr Deming was introduced into Japan by General Douglas MacArthur to lift the quality of Japanese manufactured product after the second world war.

The Third Industrial Revolution (1969)

The starting point here is the invention of the computer and the Internet and the rapid advances it allowed in the way problems were analysed and data was collected. The Internet start date is generally accepted as January 1983. The rise of computers led to networks like WAN, LAN, and at the same time robotics started to have a major impact. This in turn led to space exploration and the development of robotic technology. The use of the Internet was a big game changer in the way that data and information was handled and shared. 1973 to 1989 saw the emergence and rapid growth of digital networks, and the rapid rise of the global Internet networks. (1989 to 2004). This in turn led to more intense space exploration and the development of robotic technology.

Apple Macintosh (1984)

Figure 1.4 Apple Macintosh Computer 1984.

World Wide Web (1989)

Berners-Lee creates the world's first website.

Figure 1.5 Primitive Computer and Devices used 1989.

Figure 1.6 Artificial intelligence in Big Blue defeats world chess champion (1997). Artificial intelligence was first postulated in 1956.

The Fourth Industrial Revolution (2004)

This is all about mobility, the mobile phone, and the interlocking and melding of the physical environment with digital space. It is about the convergence of IT, the Internet of Things, big data, the cloud, machine learning digital connections, artificial intelligence, virtual reality, all imbedded in a lean manufacturing environment but applied in all parts of society including health, finance, marketing, sales, human resources, innovation, rapid research and development. This has been accelerated by advanced robotics and cognitive artificial intelligence.

Figure 1.7 Apple iPhone, 2022.

If we look at the way Industry 4.0 has generally developed in processes and manufacturing, we can identify the following stages:

1. Connecting with sensors and actuators

2. Using the connected data to add value to the value chain by re-organising and managing
3. Additional connectivity to new applications with new capabilities
4. Leveraging the new capabilities to enhance the basic goals of the business model
5. Personalisation of supply

Hence the major directions for future development could be classified as follows:

- Digitization and integration of vertical and horizontal value chains
- Digitization of products and services
- Digitized business models.
- The trend of automation and data exchange, cyber-physical systems (CPS), IoT, cloud computing, cognitive computing, and artificial intelligence

The Smart Factory

In the Smart Factory, a virtual world is created, and decentralised decisions can be made. Sensors and instrumentation drive the central forces of innovation for all elements of the industry 4.0 revolution.

In Industry 4.0 nothing goes without sensor systems.

Maintenance and fault diagnosis of machines in the future will done using virtual reality goggles where the user can home in on the problem and immediately read the solutions and methods needed to solve the issue through the glasses.

There are numerous challenges in implementing Industry 4.0 into business. These are political, social, economic, and organizational, both internally in the business and externally. However, all of these can be overcome, with the correct strategies and leadership. The business must recognise the challenge

And have a well strategized plan. In addition, there are special challenges for small businesses compared with larger enterprises.

The aerospace industry has been cited as too low in volume for industry 4.0 principles. But Aerospace parts manufacturer Meggitt PLC project M4 is a good example of how to do it. This model serves as a useful guide for all businesses.

If we look at an expanded list of industry 4.0, we have the following:

- The Internet of Things
- Wide use of sensors
- RFID technologies
- Robotics
- Mobile technologies
- Cloud computing
- Data analytics
- Big data
- Machine learning (Bayes' Law)
- Machine linking
- Artificial intelligence
- Virtual reality
- Cybersecurity
- 3D printing

Nearly all the technological elements of the fourth industrial revolution are tools to use in the framework of a good business model built on the foundations of Japanese lean manufacturing principles and advanced statistical process control. If there is no firm foundation and the leadership and culture are not harmonious and co-operative, then the total potential benefits of introducing the new Industry 4.0 ideas will not yield the benefits it should.

To achieve maximum benefit, the five functions of the business, people, operations, marketing and sales, innovation and finance, need to be integrated. This requires the judicious use of people, technology and information, and the continuous upgrading of the skills and knowledge of all. Concentration on the technical aspects of this alone will not yield the desired results. The reason for his is that the most important part of the business is the people, whether they are customers, suppliers, employees, employers or investors. Introducing new technology is easier than changing culture but they must go together.

Much of this book is based on my own consulting experience spread over 50 years in over 500 companies over 14 countries. It is important to realise that no one has all the answers and we must continue to learn from each other, but industry 4.0 gives us a new set of tools to improve ourselves and our business.

We create our own future and the parameters for this are only limited by our own imagination.

It has been estimated that artificial intelligence and automation will create in excess of $15.7 trillion in value for business over the next 10 years. Businesses that can harness the new technologies and as a result adapt and leverage these new skills will experience unprecedented growth.

This book's purpose is to describe the elements of the Fourth Industrial Revolution and illustrate what is needed to implement successfully the methods and tools and devices into business to succeed in a highly competitive global market. There is an emphasis on processes and business and manufacturing in particular. The rate of change is accelerating even more and a business we must be alert to what is necessary to remain competitive and grow. The general business principles apply to all businesses, wholesale, retail, manufacturing, and of course all those in the service industry as well. All businesses convert a raw material to a finished product using a series of processes. Here we define a process as the conversion of an input into an output. Hence even if we visit the Doctor the system involves process all of which can be driven by the new concepts of the industry 4.0 revolution.

Many medical procedures are carried out by laparoscopy. Medical procedures of this type will become more common place with the improved use of robotics and artificial intelligence as the surgeon becomes more and more an engineer. The future of digital health will theoretically extend our healthy lives as with the improved used and interpretation of all aspects of curative treatment will improve.

With all robotics or man-made devices, once the design and manufacturing problems are solved the precision with which the operations can be performed approaches a level of precision never before dreamt of. The Japanese ideas of what is called six sigma can be achieved repeatedly.

One of the major intentions of this book is to define a new way of working to the benefit of all as well as to enunciate the wonderful opportunities created by artificial intelligence in all its guises. This book aims at releasing the intellect and power of people and the new technologies and methods to achieve better customer satisfaction with faster error free integrated systems and processes.

The future for all of us looks more exciting than ever before as the full imaginative power of the human mind can be unleashed using all the tools of industry 4.0 to enhance business and human interaction.

Chapter 2

Elements of the Fourth Industrial Revolution

Summary

All of the 15 elements of the latest industry tools identified can be applied to business with very significant improvements resulting. To achieve maximum benefit, processes and systems must be controlled with a high degree of precision. The use of robotics will increase and the opportunities offered here will speed up processes and eliminate human errors. Mundane repetitive tasks for a person will be replaced by robotic techniques. The clean energy revolution will further enhance business performance and the outstanding improvements in battery technology will herald the end of the Internal combustion engine as the main means of car transportation and this will result in a cleaner healthier environment.

Modern businesses must take advantage of the opportunities offered by the appropriate industry 4.0 elements to improve and further develop their competitiveness. Too often small business owners become overwhelmed with day-to-day problems and do not recognize that if they invest in very good systems, then the "Fighting Fires" management will disappear. However, once it is recognized that a systems-based approach is necessary and that processes and systems need to operate at a very high level of

Technology for Business: Application of the Advances in Industry 4.0 to Small to Medium Sized Enterprises
John Blakemore
Copyright © 2023 Jenny Stanford Publishing Pte. Ltd.
ISBN 978-981-4968-70-6 (Hardcover), 978-1-003-38216-4 (eBook)
www.jennystanford.com

efficiency, then the issue is what is the appropriate place to start and what elements are most applicable to the immediate future development of the business. To be successful, all developments must take place within the framework of a good business structure. This structure is cultural and operational. All functions of the business must understand the transitions and changes and how it will work.

On my numerous consulting assignments, I have found that it very necessary for the CEO to be seen as leading the changes that are necessary. Therefor a clear strategy needs to be enunciated and solid clear leadership demonstrated.

The best structure to use as a basis for this is the one based on what is now called Lean Thinking which grew from the statistical work by Dr Deming in Japan after the Second World War. This approach harnesses the best of the Toyota human approach and the Honda highly mechanized approach to manufacture and the Internet of Things (IoT) and add to this the appropriate elements of the fourth industrial revolution all the elements of industry 4.0. Both the Honda and Toyota approaches must be part of enterprising leadership practicing their clear and well-defined strategy. The Honda approach is without peer in the engineering sphere as witnessed by their repeated excellence in Moto GP and now in Formula 1. In the 2021 F1 GP, Mercedes found it necessary to continually change engines to keep up with Honda engine in the Red Bull. This gave Hamilton and advantage as he only suffered a five place grid penalty for each fresh engine. Honda use Formula 1 to train their best engineers and their superior engine construction and design was significantly a factor in Verstappen winning the 2021 world championship.

Toyota and Honda advanced the Lean approach in slightly different ways but both produced products of very high quality using tightly controlled processes to a degree of precision now called Six Sigma. Six Sigma has at its core the tightness of variation so that the desired product has a variation defect rate of less than 3 parts per million. It is Dr W.E. Deming who drove this approach in Japan under General MacArthur at the end of World War 2.

The Internet of Things (IoT) may be defined as the network of connections of physical devices using a wide range of sensors or software to exchange data. This can be illustrated as shown in the following diagram. When this is understood and combined with developments based upon the Lean approach, the results are spectacular. Companies like Eurotech can offer enterprise applications for any element of Industry 4.0 and offer seamless connections to any operation.

Figure 2.1 This illustrates the breadth of the offerings that can be accessed from the Internet. This is called the Internet of Things (IoT). Using cloud computing and sharing the opportunities is endless.

If we move around the centre of this diagram, we can see that the Internet of Things covers the connections and sharing of data and information including elements of health, mechanics, music, transport, time, data, communication, mobility, ...in fact anything that can be connected via a sensor or software. IoT has led to an explosion of opportunities. It is limited only by human imagination. The systems and applications are described in detail in "internet of Things (IoT). The Elements of Industry 4.0 can be summarized as in the following table.

1	Lean	Minimum waste
2	Six Sigma	Statistical precision
3	Artificial intelligence	Attribution human skills to inanimate objects
4	AR VR	Real-world objects augmented with perceptual data
5	Big data analytics	Analysis of huge amounts of collected information
6	Cloud computing	Connection to a wide range of digital tools via IoT
7	Robotics	Automatically controlled machines
8	Connectivity	5G or other links
9	Blockchain	Encrypted interlocked records
10	Internet of Things	Digital connectivity network
11	Sensorization	Connecting devices, process linking
12	Additive manufacturing	Material added continuously to 3D object
13	Cybersecurity	Protection of data
14	Simulation	Modelling
15	Bayes rule	Machine Learning Python

Firstly, let us look at the home and common examples of devices that we use that did not exist 5 years ago. There is Alexa and Siri, for example, that can guide you in almost everything you may do. In addition, they can answer basic as well as more involved questions. These devices use artificial intelligence (AI) and the algorithms being used are continuously improving and expanding their reach. This continuous improvement is a direct result of the application of what we now know as machine learning based on what is called Bayes Rule. Robotics are being extended in reach into the everyday chores of the home. For example, iRobot is a home vacuum carpet and floor vacuum cleaner that can completely navigate the floor surface, vacuum clean it and then return to its base and empty itself. This robot is clearly mazing. The robot can move around the room with incredible precision and correct its path when the way forward is blocked, and then quickly resume vacuuming. Such clever technology will continue to be introduced into the home. The use of AI in refrigerators to measure what goes in and what goes out can become the record of your usage of food and drink and so form the basis of your next order at the supermarket. The refrigerator itself can in some models and even more in the future will diagnose any problems and notify the owner or supplier as the case may be. These trends will continue. The family car will in the future communicate directly with either the supplier or even the manufacturer to advise of service requirements or potential problems.

This musical quaver is a symbol of how we can use the IoT to play and select music scores for entertainment. Spotify can enable you to quickly find and engage your music selection and later suggest to you what other similar music you might enjoy based upon your selection. Once again, the AI algorithms will enable you to find more of the music you like faster than old techniques or personal experience or memory. This information can be regarded as big data and can be used not only to sell you more product that you may like based on past choices but can also be used to enable creators to determine which direction music appreciation is moving and so more successfully develop new products that should be in high demand. The interconnection of this with your personal profile will also help suppliers to tailor offerings in a more targeted way.

Video and film applications using CGI (Computer Graphic Imaging), are well known and the results are very exciting and very spectacular. The application of computer graphic images in art, printed media, video games, and graphic simulation. Westworld was most probably the first well known example of the early use of CGI. This was in 1973 and was followed by Star Wars. Later CGI was not constrained by what the creators believed to be the laws of physics, and this led to the creation of the virtual world of entertainment. YouTube enables us to share visual experiences at a level higher than we thought we could ever imagine.

Digital photography has added a new dimension to visual appreciation and to a large extent has enabled the average person to take photos of a much higher quality than before. All this can be done automatically with inbuilt sensors and artificial intelligence that drastically reduces the likelihood that you will take poor-quality photographs.

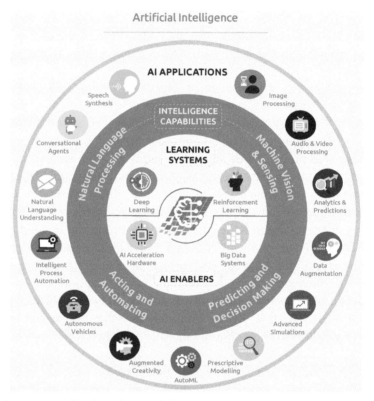

Figure 2.2 Artificial intelligence (AI) is a collective term for the capabilities shown by learning systems that are perceived by humans as representing intelligence. *Source*: Capgemini Technology, Innovation & Ventures.

Figure 2.2 is another summary to illustrate the breadth of spread of the Internet of Things (IoT) and the role of Artificial intelligence (AI). It is separated into Learning Systems and AI enablers. This is a particularly good diagram since the separation of Learning Systems and Enablers and AI applications is very clear.

The Enablers

Cloud Computing

This is the shared access to a wide range of tools both physical and virtual, on demand.

Just as computer power itself has exploded in capability, the opportunities offered by cloud computing have exploded also. It is still exponentially expanding. Wisely used the correct and most efficient say storage facility can be chosen to use as a source to drive more improvement witch never ends.

Blockchain

A blockchain is simply an encrypted interlinked set of records that is usually distributed through a series of nodes. This data can be distributed privately or publicly. In smart manufacturing a blockchain can be used to enhance supply, improve interpretation and be used for, say, transactional processes. The digital thread can be designed to be tamper proof.

Connectivity

Wireless connectivity, say through 5G, is brilliantly fast reliable and stable. Tasks in the past that were done internally in the company can be migrated the cloud and analysed or examines remotely. Thus the power is expanded exponentially.

Industrial Security

Security is simply the freedom from danger or threat. The confidentiality is preserved if the correct safeguards are in place. It is necessary to guard against sabotage, manipulation and malicious destruction.

Robotics

Automatically controlled machines that are multi-purpose and programmable to carry out a wide variety of tasks. Robotic applications continue to grow exponentially.

Augmented Reality

This is an interactive experience of a real-world environment where the objects in the real world are augmented by computer generated perceptual information. Robotics plays a key role in the advancement of AR. In summary, smart manufacturing is based on automation sensors, robotics, intelligent machines, digital twins and big data.

Simulation

Reproducing reality by modelling. This is very convenient tool for adding decision making. A very early simulation model was HOCUS, hand or computer universal simulator. Here a board model was built with counters and then this was further developed using a computer.

Additive Manufacturing

This is the manufacture by adding materials additively and continuously to produce a three-dimensional product.

Artificial Intelligence

Attribution of human skills and abilities to and inanimate object.

To fully understand the opportunities that the Internet of things can offer, it is important to understand what we mean by artificial intelligence.

Artificial intelligence can be defined as the use of tools and techniques to mimic human intelligence but doing so much faster and more accurately and with greater precision and hence less errors than humanly possible.

Winning with AI is a state of mind. Companies capturing lasting value from AI think differently from the top echelons to the frontline. The first stage is to recognize the possibilities and the run a proof of concept so that the aim of gaining lasting value can be focussed on and understood. Hence there is a scale of investment and commitment.

The AI should be aligned with the core values of the business which in turn must embrace the cultural and organization and communicational demands.

Some recent examples of the use of AI which illustrates the breadth of the possible applications include the deployment of AI in the armed forces to quickly ascertain the flightworthiness of the Black Hawk helicopter. The technique developed uses an algorithm trained on maintenance records and sensor data from the actual utilization and performance of the aircraft and then calculates how long the aircraft can fly safely in say a desert, before its engines need cleaning and further servicing.

Another example of how AI can help is the development of a screening device for cervical cancer which I was responsible for as the Chief Technologist and Research Scientist. A wand like device scans the surface of the cervix and takes a multitude if measurements which it compares with the information collected during a clinical trial. This is also an example of the use of big data to aid decision making. An algorithm is first developed based upon prior knowledge and then the device is trained to distinguish between the various lesions on the cervix and then predict the likelihood that the woman has malignant cancer. During the development of the algorithm and its refinement thousands of measurements need to be taken and compared with visual magnified images. This device is much quicker than conventional screening tests and if the data is correctly handled and the algorithm continuously refined using machine learning then sensitivity and specificity should improve. In a similar way the use of big data on COVID-19 can be used to improve the correct diagnosis of the COVID-19 infection. Sensitivity is the probability that a test result will be positive when administered to people who have the disease or condition in question.

Specificity is the probability that the test will be negative conditional that the patient is negative.

For a population with a disease, there is a normal distribution of the number of individuals and the test results. The same thing applies to those who do not have the disease. The result is two overlapping normal distributions which results in a range of false positives and false negatives. AI can be used to refine the measurement using machine learning algorithms so that the sensitivity and specificity continuously improve.

Further examples are illustrated by the way firms are using AI to forecast demands for products and services.

The expenditure of firms on Ai applications is exponential upwards. In 2017, it is believed that companies spent US$30 billion on AI related mergers and acquisitions, up by a factor of over 25 in 2 years. In addition, McKinsey reckons that just applying to marketing and sales and supply chains, could create economic value of US$40 trillion over the next 20 years.

Amazon has patented a wristband device that tracks workers hand movements of warehouse workers and using vibration to improve their efficiency. One wonders how "Moonlight Sonata "by Beethoven would sound with the degree of perfection that this device could possibly offer. Personally, I don't think it would improve this masterpiece. I have played it on my piano at least 100 times and still gasp at its beauty. Perhaps it is the absence of Six Sigma that makes it even more beautiful.

The degree of control over workers with this Amazon device is somewhat frightening. We should all think carefully about how we use Ai as individual freedom is paramount.

Usage of computer vision combined with AI will enable greater transparency and improve the efficiency and usage of safety equipment resulting in less injuries and downtime. It will also enable defence equipment to be used with even greater accuracy and precision.

Other software innovations can result in the way office layouts effect teamwork... it is limitless.

Cogito, a start-up, has deigned AI enhancing software that listens to customer calls and allocates an empathy score.

Other issues include:

- The widespread adoption of AI could put as many as 50 million jobs in Asia at risk over the next 15–20 years, with manufacturing-driven economies such as China taking most of the hit, according to research by UBS Wealth Management.
- 10 to 15 million jobs will be at risk in China as traditional business models become obsolete.
- Services-driven economies such as Hong Kong, Singapore and India, however, will probably be less affected as people still demand person to person contact.
- AI is now at the centre of a myriad of real-world applications, from facial recognition software and cyber-security to more

futuristic technologies such as autonomous self-driving vehicles.

- Chinese tech companies, including Internet heavyweights Baidu, Tencent and Alibaba group, have been pushing harder into AI to gain a leg-up before the technology has a more profound impact on people's lives.
- UBS says AI could produce economic value by introducing new product services and categories, lowering overall prices and making improvements in life styles.
- UBS predicts AI is estimated to create economic value between $US1.8 trillion and $US3 trillion a year by 2030 in Asia, and that China will see economic value between US$800 billion to US$1.25 trillion a year.
- They believe economies that can embrace AI rather than oppose it will be the ultimate beneficiaries. City states such as Hong Kong and Singapore have an edge, given their first-mover advantage and flexibility.
- AI will likely have a disproportionally high impact on financial services, healthcare, manufacturing, retail and transport industries which contribute about 66% of Asia's GDP currently.

Wide Use of Sensors

Many of us are well aware of the explosion in the use of sensors in the modern motor car for example. Sensors detecting nearness to objects on mudguards and fenders but positioned all around the car to make it safer for pedestrians and other drivers as well as the driver.

Collision avoidance technology is now common in the latest vehicles as is sensors to steer the car on a safe path on highways. There is also the LKAS system which is Lane Kerb Assist as fitted to my Honda, which steers the car on the path determined by the curve of the road.

Similarly, RFID technologies can be used to speed up processes.

Robotics

The elimination of human error in repetitive processes can be eliminated using robotic technology. Also, robots can be used in dangerous situations where life may be threatened. Early robots duplicated simple tasks but the more highly developed ones like the Honda developed ASIMO, can almost duplicate the action of a human. In modern Japanese plants autonomous robots are used to move products around. Even in the home we can use the IRobot which autonomously vacuums the floor and when the reservoir is full it finds its way home and empties itself. The major directions for future development could be classified as follows.

The major directions for the future development of the latest tools are as follows:

- Digitization and integration of vertical and horizontal value chains
- Digitization of products and services
- Digitized business models
- Trend of automation and data exchange cyber-physical systems (CPS), IoT, Cloud Computing, cognitive computing, and artificial intelligence (AI)

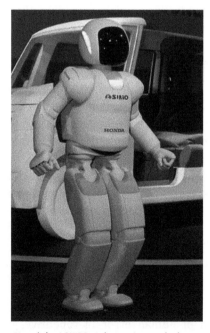

Figure 2.3 Robots. Honda's ASIMO robot, pictured above, was developed in the year 2000 and was a massive jump into the future in Robotics.

Some of the products that have been developed from the ASIMO advances are illustrated above.

Soft Botics

The science of fusing robotics into everyday life is called soft botics. The idea is to assist people in their everyday tasks using the latest digital and engineering techniques.

Soft Botics is the movement of the industrial scale application of robotics into a smaller scale. It is the movement of robotics into the home, the workplace the hospital the restaurant or the small-scale workshop.

The Smart Factory

The technologies behind the revolution occurring in manufacturing are all connected to an ever-increasing computer power associated with accelerating computational capabilities. Computer speeds and capabilities are improving drastically (Moore's law). These improvements are also a result of the following:

- Exponential growth in connectivity and sensorization.
- Faster and faster computers with increasingly speedier calculations
- Abundant data storage which is becoming increasingly cheap.
- Rapid increase in the use of batteries for storage and drives. If the new solid-state battery of Toyota comes to fruition, then a massive further revolution in solar and wind and thermal energy storage and energy distribution will take place. This could kill of the fuel cell and much of the heralded Hydrogen economy.

Added to this is the extensive use of enablers like artificial intelligence, virtual and augmented reality, cloud computing, simulation, collaborative robotics, blockchain and data analytics, and the Internet of Things.

The net result of the application of these is what is called product personalization, circular manufacturing, and data driven businesses. This will lead to what is called servitization, which offers the possibility to add additional service products to a physical product.

With circular manufacturing, products will be more sustainable. Used products can be recycled and refurbished and may be rebuilt. With extensive use of data analytics collected during its use the next generation of the product will be enhanced and many features improved with continuous customer feedback.

As we shift from traditional to smart manufacturing, it is accepted that the greatest success will be achieved if the parties collaborate constructively and more effectively. This means collaboration between supplier, producer and customer at all parts in the supply chain. It is the integration of systems and processes.

The secret here is to accurately produce a digital model which replicates the real situation. This is where in many instances art and science separate.

All the enablers such as the Internet of Things, additive manufacturing, simulation, enhanced connectivity, blockchain and robotics can be leveraged effectively with the correct strategy.

It will be possible also to have all automation and real time control in the cloud and this sometimes referred to as edge computing.

Smart manufacturing is the immediate future. The faster a company incorporates the new ideas and applies them to their lean business framework the more competitive it will become.

In the smart factory a virtual world is created and decentralized decisions can be made.

Sensors and instrumentation drive the central forces of innovation for all elements of the industry 4.0 revolution.

In Industry 4.0 nothing goes without sensor systems.

Maintenance and fault diagnosis of machines in the future will done using virtual reality (VR), goggles where the user can home in on the problem and immediately read the solutions and methods needed to solve the issue through the glasses.

There are numerous challenges in implementing Industry 4.0 into business. These are political, social, economic, and organizational, both internally in the business and externally. However, all of these can be overcome, with the correct strategies and leadership.

In addition, there are special challenges for small businesses compared with larger enterprises.

The aerospace industry has been cited as too low in volume for industry 4.0 principles. But Aerospace parts manufacturer Meggitt PLC project M4 is a good example of how to do it.

Hydrogen and Environmentally Friendly Energy

It was only 5 years ago that the E Car and the Hydrogen fuel cell car looked like they could be equivalent and each one would be a worthy competitive rival for the other. Both Honda and Toyota backed the fuel cell. The reasons given by Honda were legitimate. Their attitude was that the electric car would get its charging energy from large power stations which were not nuclear powered and were predominately powered by fossil fuels like coal. Therefore in the total supply chain the fuel cell was more environmentally friendly than the battery powered electric car. Others like Tesla backed battery technology. It is now clear that with the recent very significant advances in battery efficiency that the fuel cell has lost the battle and Honda and Toyota have lost ground on their competitors. Honda have now belatedly forged an alliance with Sony and Toyota are developing a solid-state battery to compete. This area is exploding with innovation and it is not clear who will join Tesla as the second in line with Eco friendly cars. The Chinese with BYD (Build Your Dreams), could soon be number 2 with their blade battery.

Ammonia Fuel Cell

It is expected that if the problems associated with the ammonia (NH3) fuel cell are overcome, then this will provide another low emission transport solution and this will also overcome the difficulties associated with hydrogen liquification and storage, both of which are enormously costly. The ammonia fuel cell if successful will revolutionise the transport industry not only for cars but for large ships and even aircraft.

In addition, to power a hydrogen fuel cell car, the supply chain has a number of steps as shown below. The battery powered electric car is far simpler.

Hydrogen fuel cell car

1. Energy generation
2. Electrolysis
3. Liquefaction
4. Transportation and filling
5. Fuel cell power generation
6. Electric battery (low capacity)
7. E engine

Battery powered E car

1. Energy generation
2. Transportation and storage
3. Electric battery high capacity
4. E engine

Clearly the battery-powered car is a simpler solution.

Tesla have invested heavily in high pressure aluminium diecasting operations for the framework of their cars. One factory planned for Germany will produce 1,000,000 cars per year. This is an exceptionally bold move. The high-powered high-pressure diecasting machines employed are a world apart from the previous generation of high-pressure aluminium diecasting machines.

Chinese manufacturer BYD (Build Your Dreams) has developed the blade battery which offers superior recharging rates and less chance of catching fire.

Nearly all the technological elements of the fourth industrial revolution are tools to use in the framework of a good business model built on the foundations of Japanese lean manufacturing principles and advanced statistical process control.

We create our own future and the parameters for this are only limited by our imagination.

This book's sole purpose is to describe the elements of the vague term the Fourth Industrial Revolution and illustrate what is needed to implement successfully the methods and tools and devices into business to succeed in a highly competitive global market. The rate of change is accelerating even more, and a business must be alert to what is necessary to remain competitive and grow.

Chapter 3

Culture Leadership and Strategic Planning

Summary

The introduction of the technology of industry 4.0 into any environment results in a significant change in the way things are done. Change is not always easy. To be successful it must be led from the top of the organisation and a firm well-articulated strategic plan understood and implemented. There are two major parts to the change process, slow improvement, kaizen, and step function change, major innovation. The readiness for change will depend on the culture of the organisation and the quality of the leadership of the change process.

3.1 The People Process

Business is about people, process and precision. Businesses of the future will produce to-demand with small batch sizes and maybe to a batch size of one. Precision of process in all business functions at "Six Sigma" tightness of control creates a strong competitive advantage. Technology and process improvements are advancing at an increasing rate. As a result,

Technology for Business: Application of the Advances in Industry 4.0 to Small to Medium Sized Enterprises
John Blakemore
Copyright © 2023 Jenny Stanford Publishing Pte. Ltd.
ISBN 978-981-4968-70-6 (Hardcover), 978-1-003-38216-4 (eBook)
www.jennystanford.com

new pressures are placed on management and leadership, if they want the enterprise to grow and be competitive. Global supply chains with networks of suppliers feeding strategically placed assembly plants near the market they serve are commonplace, especially in big business.

A key question is how do small businesses, both in manufacturing and service, take advantage of the new and efficient cooperative ways of satisfying customers, with higher expectations, faster than before?

This book offers the solution to this familiar challenge to management ... faster innovation, product and service delivery at a higher-degree of precision ... Six Sigma processes using lean thinking and digital data from the source.

Research requires mental agility. As a result of this – along with the cooperation of over 400 clients both in Australia and overseas and a career dedicated to learning from the best – I have developed 26 rules to analyse and implement lean systems (26 Rules for Lean Systems) and 22 creative ideas to aid innovation of process and product (22 Creative Ideas for Innovation). These have been applied with considerable success, and some of my programs are discussed later.

With the experience of over 900 reports and papers, and numerous innovations and awards by over 400 clients in eight countries, as well as the saving of my own eyesight by applying the 22 Creative Ideas for Innovation described here, I feel confident enough to write this book. I hope all businesses can benefit as my clients have done.

The first three fundamental characteristics of good business practice are quality, cost and delivery aimed at exceeding customer expectations. Add to this innovation and speed with a special focus on continuous improvement. Continuous research and development of both process and product is fundamental. It is clear that to achieve best practice we should have total cooperation in all of the supply chain to achieve maximum benefit for all participants. Cooperating to compete is a strong competitive advantage.

Digital connections to suppliers and customers will assist in making companies more agile. Some innovative companies have clearly demonstrated how the new rules can work very effectively.

With the new digital cooperative lean approach, value-adding by decreasing waste in planning, process and expenses continuously increases as we innovate. Digital connections allow companies to move and use information anywhere along the supply chain. This allows any enterprise in the chain to more accurately forecast or ultimately Make-To-Order (MTO) only.

Such ideas will not work to advantage if the processes are not operating at a high-degree of precision; a level that is now regarded as processes at such a level of reduced variation that the defect rate outside the range of acceptability for the customer is only 3.0 parts per million. Variation in process is a major enemy of speed.

To achieve maximum benefit, the five functions of business – people, operations, marketing and sales, innovation and finance – need to be integrated. This requires the judicious use of people, technology and information, and the continuous training and upgrading of people skills and knowledge. Concentration on the technical aspects of these factors alone will not yield the desired results. The reason is that the most important part of all business is people, whether they are customers, employees, employers or investors. Introducing new technology and techniques is much easier than changing culture and behaviour, but they must go together.

In the early stages of a business transformation, use of simple management tools can lead to significant productivity gains in bottleneck areas of the system, and these can be used as a guide to assist in culture change and further innovations. This is clearly practiced at the plants of Japanese clients I have worked with over the years; companies like Panasonic, Matsushita, Canon, Honda, Toyota and Kawai. Special mention is made in this book of the work of Honda and their BP (Best Position, Productivity, Product, Price, Partners) Program. Honda has a very special place in my heart and mind because of the supremely high standard of their engine integrity and the fast innovation they apply to linking process and product innovation. They had none of the earlier financial support that Toyota had, and yet have excelled.

When we come to the actual process of changing a bad enterprise into a good one, it is important to realise that you can only go so far in improving culture if all that is changed is the physical environment. If the culture is poor, then physical improvements may result in substantial improvement that can be quickly eroded by a poor Management Team.

This book's core message has developed around 30 years of consulting to management. It takes the latest principles relating to what is commonly called Lean Manufacturing and Total Quality Management (TQM) with the latest management principles, and focuses on compressing supply chains and identifying an improved competitive advantage, the velocity of the processes and systems and therefore it provides the best foundation for further development using the tools of industry 4.0.

3.2   The Role of Management

It is important to understand that the methods described are proven, scientific and logical, but their successful implementation will not work without the support and leadership of a good Management Team. The culture and vision of this team and the company is set by the Chief Executive Officer, Senior Management and the Board. The basic thesis is that western-style management has recognised the superior performance of many Japanese companies, such as Toyota, Honda, Panasonic and Canon and has attempted to duplicate their formula with (in many cases) a high-degree of failure, particularly for American automotive manufacturers. Why? In almost all cases in the literature, the reason is associated with the people function, leadership and culture, not the technology or technical techniques.

Successful modern management involves a sharp customer focus and the rapid use of high-quality information via digital computer systems that are conveyed through a network of teams in a compressed hierarchical structure. The organisational structure must allow creativity, communication, improvement and innovation of all processes and functions. Companies must plan for the long-term and plans should be continually updated.

People must be rewarded for creativity, communication skills and continuous improvement and innovation. The focus is on precision, speed and quality in the entire supply chain. Cross-functionality, innovation and fast financial management within a short time period must be core elements of production and serving customers. The enterprise now must be an integrated structure of people driving innovation to satisfy and exceed customer needs and wants. Measurements of processes and systems must be at the source of the activity, and the financial outcomes must be available quickly. Digital data can satisfy this need. Financial data should be available quickly, but looked upon as real-time output.

It is vital that modern managers understand reporting as well as communication, budgeting and the full implications of profit and loss accounts, balance sheets and cashflow. They must also understand the concept of continuous research and development, training, education, and never-ending improvement. The Board sets the strategy, direction and philosophy that will drive the mindset of managers in the future where innovation, a sharp customer focus, flexibility and speed are urgently needed for all people, processes and systems.

New tools and techniques, such as the 26 Rules for Lean Systems for process improvement and for innovation of process, the 22 Creative Ideas for Innovation will assist management in championing the new approach.

It is the intention of this book to enunciate a new interpretation of the management processes and systems to facilitate a more caring and successful human side to work. This book aims to release the intellect and power of the people and realise the potential of producing to-demand with a batch size of one. It is about high-velocity integrated systems driven by innovative caring management.

3.3   Western Style Management

Set in a world context, overall performance of manufacturing in USA and Australia over the last 30 years has the following elements, all of which are contributing to their difficulties:

- Inability to commercialise its own Intellectual Property (Australia only)
- A failure to capitalise on our natural comparative advantages (USA and Australia)
- A management philosophy that is short-term (USA and Australia)
- A focus on the local market only and a blurred focus on export of value-added goods – high value-added manufactured goods are called Elaborately Transformed Manufactures (ETMs) by the Australian Bureau of Statistics (see US Auto Industry)
- Poor labour flexibility
- Continuing high cost of production
- Low expenditure on research and development (Australia only)
- An inordinate degree of protection (Australia only)
- Soaring charges for distribution
- The difficulty in moving goods in and out of ports (addressed in 2000) (Australia only)
- Application of outmoded technology (Australia only)
- A failure of universities to produce graduates interested in manufacturing (Australia only)
- Too long a chain of decision-making in industrial corporations (USA and Australia)
- A tax system that makes investment in manufacturing less attractive than, for example, real estate (Australia only)

3.4   Japanese Style Management

Athos and Pascale in 1981 published the classic "The Art of Japanese Management" and studied Matsushita and Honda in some detail. They isolated a seven-part framework around which Japanese management is structured. These seven points are given in Table 3.1 with a note based on my experience in Japan, with Matsushita in particular.

Table 3.1 Seven-part framework

No	Framework	Focus
1.	Strategy	Operations, customer, manufacturability, cost
2.	Structure	Mixed centralised and decentralised
3.	Systems	Precision and customer
4.	Style	Values and honesty
5.	Subordinate goals	Targets
6.	Sequencing	Timing and implementation
7.	Skill	Centralised training

Based on the above and my experience in Japan, the keys to Japanese success are as follows:

- Application of the scientific method and logical deduction to achieve precision in process and product ... i.e. the application of the basic statistical principles introduced to Japan by Dr. Deming after the second world war, i.e. what is now known as Six Sigma. This is used extensively to solve production and marketing problems and in fact in all functions of the business, it is not confined to manufacturing although this is where it began. This in turn led to a control system emphasising process not product alone and then to new ways of measuring the financial performance of the company.

- Management by consensus, where possible. Perfect consensus is impossible but retrieving a collective input from a larger number of inputs leads generally to a better result but more importantly to a result where the people felt that their opinion is valued and they have been listened to so the chances of successful implementation is enhanced.

- Rapid application of new technology – innovation, both breakthrough or disruptive and Kaizen as illustrated by slow continuous improvement.

- A continuous desire to improve incrementally, as described by Masaaki Imai.

- An emphasis on:
  - Teamwork
  - Continuous value-adding
  - Lean manufacturing (continuous flow)
  - Process innovation
  - Training and education
  - Statistics and Statistical Process Control (SPC)
  - Quality assurance
  - Continuous focus on integrating processes to add to the velocity of the system

The above points can be summarised in terms of creative innovation using the principles of lean manufacturing; continuous flow, and using statistical methods embedded by Dr. Deming in "Out of the Crisis", and Dr. Shewhart in "Economic Control of Quality of Manufactured Product", and utilised throughout the whole of the supply chain.

Over the last 60 years, amazing advances have been made by Japan in increasing quality and productivity. Toyota, after establishing its first plant in the USA in 1970, now dominates the US Auto Industry and – as early as the Financial Year 2003 to 2004 – made a net profit of US$11.4 billion; enough to buy GM and Ford combined. But why would they? Look at what happened in 2008 during the GFC. Since then, Toyota has suffered a drop in quality as a result of management changes in Tokyo. No such aberration occurred with Honda.

The Japanese have proved that by increasing quality you can increase productivity – a concept that was anathema to western management even 30 years ago. Aajime Karatsu, Managing Director of Matsushita Communication, stated that, 'As the quality increases, the cost of production decreases'. He also stated that strict inspection is 'not to be proud of'. He claims as well that the number of breakdowns decreases as the process is improved; the operation rate increases and the cost is further reduced.

Results of my own analysis in over 400 companies over 30 years fit well with those of Dr. Deming and have yielded the following:

- In excess of 75% of productivity problems can be traced to the system and management – Dr. Deming claims 85% of the problems are due to the system.
- Less than 20% of productivity problems can be traced directly to the workers or machines – Dr. Deming claims 15%.
- Management must commit itself to production methods and quality standards.
- The control of quality must start at the top of the management hierarchy to be successful, but a successful quality system involves everyone.
- Adequate control of quality and productivity can lead to a reduction in operating costs of between 20% and 50%.
- Reasonable people will probably accept a quality system based upon consensus – such a system makes Japanese workers more reliable, conscientious, diligent and smart.
- The west must improve its productivity of value-adding activities.

Based upon my own experience in Australia and numerous other countries, there is ample evidence to suggest the popularly held belief that the cultural, religious and class regimentation of the Japanese is more suited to high-productivity could be true, and therefore to apply the new philosophy requires a change in attitudes, beliefs, behaviour and leadership for it to work in western countries. Nevertheless, it will work in our culture.

In particular, the outstanding success of the Sony Corporation in San Diego using American workers and Japanese methods is living proof that the western world can do it. In addition, a 100% success rate for process innovation programs based upon Japanese manufacturing management techniques, run by myself in Australia, further confirms it.

Management must totally understand that the consumer is the most important part of the production line. Japanese management stands behind its products' performance and is continually looking forward to design and development of new products, unlike western management. Using lean thinking, Honda had reduced its development time for a new car from clean sheet of paper to world launch to 36 months (Honda Integra). Honda has reverted to a five-year cycle for other reasons.

A successful product development plan involves an accurate analysis of the marketplace and a scientific approach. Too often we are myopic. We look at short-term gain for long-term penalty. We too often judge on the size of the next annual dividend. This should not be considered to be as important as the continuation of the business in ten years' time.

Dr. Deming's 14 points for management of the new philosophy are discussed in detail in this book and have already been expanded for the US culture by Jeffery K. Liker in "The Toyota Way: 14 Management Principles from the World's greatest Manufacturer".

Reasons for Adopting Industry 4.0 Principles

1. Increased productivity with less errors and defective products and relationships.
2. Decreased cost of operations as steps in the value chain are reduced and waste is eliminated.
3. The opportunity for increased innovation.
4. Improved employee and employer and customer relations.
5. Improved communication and less ambiguity.
6. Improved customer satisfaction.

For a successful application, the industry 4.0 elements need a solid Lean framework in which to operate.

3.5   The Lean Framework

At first glance the explosion of knowledge and opportunities presented by continuous acceleration of new knowledge and the exponential waves of new opportunities this creates appears to be overwhelming. However, once you have devised a strategy and have a framework in place to grow the business further, the introduction of the new ideas becomes much easier.

The rules of Lean are simple. They are:

1. Produce only what you can sell, i.e. make to order always if possible. If the lead time is greater than acceptable to the customer, then we must make to a forecast, but if this is the case, then we still must keep our inventory and hence working capital to a minimum.

2. Minimise waste in all forms. Typical waste areas that can be easily improved are space, inventory, errors and rework, defects, design errors, setup times, idle times, excess batch sizes, etc.

We must plan for agility. his strategy must fall within an agile framework. The most successful framework within which these new ideas will prosper is one based on the Lean thinking philosophy.

The term Lean was first coined from a study of the World's automotive manufacturing, which was a study of the world's leading automobile manufacturers instituted by the US government and it became known as the International Motor Vehicle Program (IMVP). This program was created by Massachusetts Institute of Technology in the USA in 1979 and through education and implementation revolutionised the production of motor vehicles in the USA and the world. It has now flowed on to all manufacturing and later to all types of businesses.

The word Lean was used because the obvious difference between western manufacturing plants and Japanese ones was the fact that there was no waste space or inventory or movement in the Japanese plants compared with the USA plants. This to a large extent was the result of Japanese isolation and obsession with perfection of the Japanese Samurai warrior. Japan is predominately mountainous, and space is limited if it is to house 123 million in 1990 or 77 million in 1945. Much of the success of Japan as an industrial powerhouse rests on a technique called Kaizen. This literally means change for good.

Kaizen

Many people have summarised the Kaizen philosophy as small incremental improvements but Kaizen can also lead to massive step function change. In fact, the massive step function changes do not become observable until much of the kaizen approach is completed.

A good example of this thinking was on display when I visited the Canon plant in Toride, Japan, in 2007. Canon were developing a new printing press which became known as the Omnipress. Much of the first stages of commercialisation and the usage of this unique machine was done in Sydney at North Ryde. The philosophy of this was to produced books in the smallest batch size as possible, in fact in a batch size of one. I was fortunate to work with the team in Sydney and we did in fact produce my book "Velocity" in a batch size of one. Inventory could be almost eliminated. The idea was to produce the multi covered covers printed in advance but have the text on a disc or pen-drive and simply have the covers in a tray linked to the machine, press a button and the whole book would be printed and bound with the cover on in the space of a few minutes. This is a good example of how the industry 4.0 concept of digital printing and supply chain compression can save space and money.

I imagined that in the future we could walk into a bookstore and see the book of our choicer but then wait a few minutes while the vendor printed and bound a copy from the Omnipress. So far, the machine has only found use in the wholesale area not the retail arena.

3.6   Elements of Industry 4.0

Reasons for adopting Industry 4.0 Principles

1. Increased productivity with less errors and defective products and relationships
2. Decreased cost of operations as steps in the value chain are reduced and waste is eliminated
3. The opportunity for increased innovation
4. Improved employee and employer and customer relations
5. Improved communication and less ambiguity
6. Improved customer satisfaction

Internet of Things (IoT)

Modern businesses must take advantage of the opportunities offered by the appropriate industry 4.0 element to improve and further develop their competitiveness. All these developments must take place within the framework of a good lean structure harnessing the best of the Toyota human approach and the Honda highly mechanised approach.

Internet of Things (IoT). Toyota and Honda advanced the Lean approach in slightly different ways but both produced products of very high quality.

The Internet of Things (IoT) may be defined as the network of connections of physical devices using a wide range of sensors or software to exchange data. This can be illustrated as in the following diagram.

Figure 3.1 The Internet of Things.

If we move around the centre, we can see that it covers the connections and sharing of data and information covering elements of health, mechanics, music, transport, time, data, communication, mobility, ... in fact anything that can be connected via a sensor or software. IoT has led to an explosion of opportunities. It is limited only by human imagination. The systems and applications are described in detail in "Internet of Things (IoT)" (5).

Wide Use of Sensors

Many of us are well aware of the explosion in the use of sensors in the modern motor car. Sensors detecting nearness to objects on mudguards and fenders but positioned all around the car to make it safer for pedestrians and other drivers as well as the driver. Collision avoidance technology is now common in the latest vehicles as is sensors to steer the car on a safe path on highways. Similarly, RFID technologies can be used to speed up processes.

Use of On-line Platforms

The usage of on-line Internet platforms like Zoom, Teams and Skype is becoming widespread. These are wonderful tools for peer-to-peer learning despite some inherent disadvantages.

Listening to Customers

Use of digital platforms has led to a revolution in the way businesses are interacting with customers. A good example of the way businesses are interacting in the value chain and the changes that this makes are best illustrated by the new Agency concept for selling cars being implemented by Honda. The further you are away from the source, the customer the more distorted the message. Honda have recognised that the dealer network is insulating them from the true voice of the customer so they have responded with a new model.

Dealers can no longer set the price to the customer. This is set by Honda and no discounts are allowed. Previously Dealers were often bidding against themselves for sales. This will disappear with Agency model. In addition, the capital invested in the real estate of the dealerships will be reduced and much of the customer education and model knowledge will be promulgated over the Internet. This releases more money for research and development. Warranties will be more tightly controlled as will the training and development of the service personnel. All this should mean greater customer satisfaction. Since the Agency relationship will be controlled by Honda, the sharing of information between agencies and Honda should improve. The result should be faster customer feedback and solution to problems or speedier further innovation. It will be interesting to see how German companies in particular respond and what this will do to brand capital. In all, cases this concept should help bridge the IT gap between the customer and the factory floor ... always a pet grievance of mine where the person I had to deal with after my car was serviced could not adequately answer my questions. With the introduction of the Agency system the dealer I was using to service my car lost his dealership and I was forced to do to another and suddenly I discovered that the first dealer was not doing all the service work correctly. With the new Agency model this should not happen. As well there will be a greater personalisation of supply.

Artificial Intelligence

Artificial intelligence originally was defined as the development of digital computer-based techniques to perform human tasks. These tasks currently include visual perception, speech recognition, advanced decision making, translation. Broadly speaking it includes machine learning. It is the way data is collected and used intelligently to achieve a desired objective. Latest developments include virtual reality (VR).

Sensors

We are now living in a world where every move is being measured or monitored. This leads to massive data acquisition and feedback and for business the opportunity for the further use of machine vision and for manufacturing applications the use of Statistical Process Control (SPC).

Cloud Computing

Cloud computing is on demand availability of computer system resources especially data storage and computer power and knowledge sources. It is a data centre available over the Internet and operates in real time and is available on demand.

Data Analytics and Big Data

The ability to collect data digitally and at light speed enables huge amount of data to be collected to assist in solving problems.

A good example of the use of big data is the collection of multi-spot measurements on the cervix of a woman patient using a sensitive scanning device and immediately feeding this to data base for thousands of women and hen instantaneously assessing whether she has cervical cancer or not. In this case during the setup stage for the device machine learning algorithms based on Bayes Law were used to refine the measuring tool sensitivity.

Another example is the use of the analysis of big data to predict stock market trends. Literally tens of thousands of stocks can be analysed in real time for a large number of parameters such as market cap, div yield, P/E, Peer position, weighted mean average, and many other parameters.

Big Data and analytics have given birth to what is now called smart services. These are products of the 21st Century. Google and Amazon sell smart services rather than anything physical. Netflix and Spotify are also examples of smart services. In both of these cases they give instant access to a very wide range ranging library of content.

The power of big data and analytics can best be illustrated by the case of the digital data used by Cambridge Analytica to have a significant influence on the election of Donald Trump to the Presidency of the United States.

Machine Learning (Bayes Law)

One of the most useful tools in the digital arsenal for big data and data analytics is the use of Bayes Law in real time. This means that the algorithm is continuously refining itself to become more accurate.

Bayes and at the same time Laplace both postulated this method but now it is greatly in favour.

Figure 3.2 Thomas Bayes (1701–1761) on the left and Pierre-Simon Laplace (1749–1827), the fathers of Bayes Law.

Mobile Technologies

Mobile technologies have now developed to such a degree that as we all know we can access our bank accounts and other on-line data almost anywhere in real time. The ubiquitous iPhone and its equivalents are now always with us and are indispensable.

Six Sigma

With the rise of machine-to-machine connections and on-line communication, the importance of accuracy cannot be overstressed.

3D printing

The application of artificial intelligence and the on-demand interpretation of data has led to the invention of 3D printing.

Cybersecurity

Mobility and digitisation of data has led to a massive increased risk. Once the information is in the digital space, who knows where it ends up. I thought this would make people more honest, but maybe the converse is true.

Immediate Everyday Results of the Current Use of Industry 4.0 Concepts

Innovation on Display

There is no better arena for studying rapid innovation than Formula 1 for cars and Moto GP for motorcycles.

The modern F1 car is an example of the latest thinking in moving a powered vehicle at high speed with maximum safety. It places tremendous strain on the Driver and the Pitt crew.

Engine technology continues to evolve with turbo charging, energy savings devices and new ways of controlling the flow of air around the vehicle. The innovation never stops.

The continuous improvement flows into the every-day motor vehicle as most of the significant advances were made I the F1 arena.

The following will serve as examples of rapid innovation.

Red Bull Honda 2021

A good example of how one innovation can lead to many other innovations is well illustrated by the following series of developments.

The Honda engine in the Red Bull is HCC I, i.e. Homogeneous Charge Compression Ignition. It therefore critically important all aspects of the combustion process are under tight control, Six Sigma control and precision. F1 is about looking for more speed and efficiency continuously. Their latest innovation led to a substantial comparative advantage compared with their main rival, Mercedes. The sequence of innovations is listed below:

1. Honda applied the Kumamoto coating to the walls of the cylinders to decrease friction. This innovation was a direct result of the work done by the Motorcycle Division. There was a drop in temperature as a result of this.
2. This enabled Honda to move the cylinders closer together.
3. This meant the size and weight of the engine block decreased and the heat and recovery systems could be improved. These were improved with help of the HondaJet division.
4. All the above meant that the centre of gravity was lowered.
5. This in turn led to the backend of the chassis being lowered.

6. As a result of this, the rear fin was redesigned and the car we believe had less drag and better downforce control.

Figure 3.3 The winner of the F1 drivers title in 2021 Max Verstappen in the Honda powered Red Bull. With any reasonable luck he would have won the championship by over 50 points.

The Red Bull Honda became the fastest F1 car on the circuit. However, in the rapidly innovative arena of F1 each manufacturer jumps over the other repeatedly. Mercedes responded quickly but the edge given to Red Bull did result in Verstappen becoming the F1 champion in 2021 despite all the controversy he is the worthy winner.

The rapid use of sensors and digital information combined with the high precision of manufactured parts to Six Sigma standards, and the use of algorithms with machine learning accelerated the development and application of these innovations.

It worth noting as well the cooperative effort of the 3 Honda divisions in achieving their goal, aerospace, general mechanical and motor vehicles.

The Smart Factory

In the Smart Factory a virtual world is created and decentralised decisions can be made.

Sensors and instrumentation drive the central forces of innovation for all elements of the industry 4.0 revolution.

In Industry 4.0 nothing goes without sensor systems.

Maintenance and fault diagnosis of machines in the future will done using VR goggles where the user can home in on the problem and immediately read the solutions and methods needed to solve the issue through the glasses.

There are numerous challenges in implementing Industry 4.0 into business. These are political, social, economic, and organizational, both internally in the business and externally. However, all of these can be overcome, with the correct strategies and leadership. The business must recognise the challenge.

And have a well strategized plan.

In addition, there are special challenges for small businesses compared with larger enterprises.

The aerospace industry has been cited as too low in volume for industry 4.0 principles. But Aerospace parts manufacturer Meggitt PLC project M4 is a good example of how to do it. This model serves as a useful guide for all businesses.

Nearly all the technological elements of the fourth industrial revolution are tools to use in the framework of a good business model built on the foundations of Japanese lean manufacturing principles and advanced statistical process control.

We create our own future and the parameters for this are only limited by our own imagination.

Chapter 4

People, Quality and Industry 4.0

Summary

People are the most important part of business, whether it be customers, staff, suppliers. To be truly successful, the business must harness the full potential of all its natural talent. The people must believe in the vision and the strategy on how to achieve the company's objectives at the same time as the individual achieves theirs. The tools of industry 4.0 can only be used effectively if they are applied in the correct strategic areas of the business which will make a positive difference to the culture and the bottom line. Japanese management techniques have been shown to be superior to western management methods and in the world of the latest industry 4.0 tools the lean framework established in Japan is fundamental.

4.1 People

The most important asset in a business is people. There are a number of special, well-established features about people in business as discussed by McGregor, Ouchi, Brown, and more recently Akerlof and Shiller. The work of Elton Mayo needs consideration, since the Hawthorne Effect is real. People want to be loved.

Technology for Business: Application of the Advances in Industry 4.0 to Small to Medium Sized Enterprises
John Blakemore
Copyright © 2023 Jenny Stanford Publishing Pte. Ltd.
ISBN 978-981-4968-70-6 (Hardcover), 978-1-003-38216-4 (eBook)
www.jennystanford.com

The fundamental observations regarding Total Quality Management (TQM), made by Konosuke Matsushita (Founder of Matsushita Electric Industrial Co. – renamed Panasonic) and Dr. Deming hold as true today as ever they were. Konosuke Matsushita made the very brave statement in 1950:

> "We are going to win and the industrial west is going to lose out. There is nothing much you can do about it because the reasons for your failure are within yourselves. Your firms are built on the Taylor model; even worse so are your heads with your bosses doing the thinking while the workers wield the screwdrivers, you are convinced deep down that this is the right way to run a business."

For anyone like me who has dealt directly with Panasonic, these words have a solid ring, but many western businesses have responded.

As an example of their commitment to the customer, the following experience I had with Panasonic is worth recording. In 1985, I was asked to investigate a VHS video duplication problem at The Duplication Centre in Sydney. The CEO had complained that all the Panasonic machines were breaking down and were unreliable. Upon investigation, I found the units were failing at 2,500 to 3,000 hours of operation. The maintenance handbook specified preventive maintenance at 1500 hours, but this was not done. The Duplication Centre had run the machines into the ground. At my request, Panasonic sent three Japanese engineers from Osaka to work with me. We completely rebuilt all the machines but with the statement that the preventative maintenance at 1,500 hours should be done and that the machines were now as good as new. There was no charge to the customer.

This is an example of extreme customer dedication.

I have had a similar experience with Honda who replaced an Electronic Control Unit (ECU) at 120,000 km free of charge, despite the fact that the car was out of warranty. There was no charge and the replacement took place at a normal service interval.

Dell, in the past, was regarded by numerous Harvard professors, such as McFarlane and Yoshino and Professor Williams from INSEAD when I attended their lectures, as a pointer to the way of future manufacturing. They are, of course, correct provided that Dell control the quality of process and product of their sub-contractors and suppliers. These experts failed to mention how important the quality of process and product is to the Made to Order (MTO) model. This system is brilliant if the processes and systems operate at a Six Sigma level. Unfortunately, the component parts in the Dell computer supplied to me were of inferior quality. I now run a full Apple Macintosh system. This is, so far, trouble-free and a joy to use.

As mentioned, people are the enterprise's most important asset. The question is: How do we all work together for the common good so that both the company and the individual achieve their goals? The most important person in the supply chain is the customer.

As a first step along the way, it is important to realise that, in the near future, the organisational structure of successful companies will be core process-based, not based on vertical silos. The new structure is illustrated in Figure 4.1. This Venn diagram is designed to illustrate that all functions in businesses overlap. Digital information flow cuts across all functional boundaries.

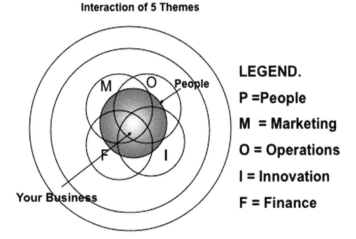

Business Environment

Interaction of 5 Themes

LEGEND.

P =People

M = Marketing

O = Operations

I = Innovation

F = Finance

Figure 4.1 The new organisation.

Many analysts have attempted to prioritise the elements of people power. The most likely acceptable priority of the people groups, if the enterprise is to be successful, is as follows:

- The customer
- The staff
- The shareholder

The key in future will be to team-up with suppliers and customers in a mutually beneficial partnership – reward each other appropriately and cooperate to achieve high-quality and high-velocity. It is about networking to achieve precision and velocity and cooperating to compete with agile tight precise processes and systems.

Organisations should recognise that all major functions in a business have to play a collaborative role. The vertical silo approach has serious limitations. Figure 4.1 is designed to illustrate that no major function is independent of any other. If we are going to get the best out of people, then the organisation that understands how the integration of all functions can work will win in the future.

Anything that happens anywhere in a company has an effect on all the other functions. Understanding this link is critical to the future success of any business. This goes even further and extends to the whole of the supply chain, called pipelining. Integration is the key to achieving maximum velocity for maximum customer satisfaction. We can achieve seamless integration with the correct use of digital data and agile system. Vertical functional silos are replaced with overlapping functions and responsibilities as illustrated.

To be successful, we must realise that we are probably only one step in a supply chain. We must create value for all participants. If your partners are unsuccessful, then this will have a devastating effect on you. A section of the supply chain is schematically illustrated in Figure 4.2.

All participants are dependent on each other. The objective is to collaborate to generate value for all. Note the two elements in the chain are virtual (digital information) and physical (tangible goods and services). The virtual layer can travel at the speed of light, but the physical layer is dependent on a range of variables, and can be optimised and risk-minimised.

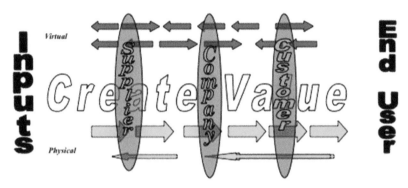

Figure 4.2 Supply chain for tangible goods and services and digital data.

We must aim for a physical lead-time 100% value-added in all processes and systems. An impossible goal, but what is the limit? Service value is created and measured by the customer at the buying decision interface. All elements or themes or functions influence the success or otherwise of this event.

All major functions in the business have a role to play at the buying decision stage, as shown in Figure 4.3. As Sun Tzu stated in his classic "The Art of War", strategy without tactics will lead to a slow victory, but tactics without strategy will lead to defeat. Once the decision is made to buy, the core processes of the enterprise must create a product or service delivering customer value for the highest level of customer satisfaction, customer loyalty and potential repeat business. All systems are affected by the strategic decisions made to capitalise on opportunities and create a competitive advantage and improve organisational effectiveness.

If a broad view of the supply chain (value chain) is taken, it can be seen that decisions in any one part of the chain – either internal or external – have very wide ramifications. The overall message is that the success of the total operation is dependent on all the steps in the chain. The aim is to satisfy the customers 100% of the time in quality, cost and delivery. The more flexible the process, the shorter the lead-time and the shorter the planning cycle can be.

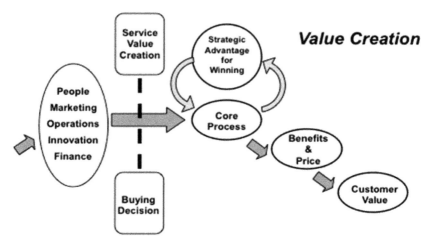

Figure 4.3 Strategic chain.

At less than 2% process value-added – where many companies are – there is plenty of room for improvement. With the introduction of Business to Business (B2B) in future, the system velocity will increase, but be very dependent on the quality of process and product. It is possible to operate on a Reverse Purchase Order (RPO) system that – when designed for the supply of Speedo male swimming costumes to Myer in Melbourne – can produce unexpectedly positive results and increased sales.

The plan is to operate the production in the early stages on replacement and minimum stock levels using kanban cards. On the raw material supply side for long lead-times, a forecasting system will still be used with a focus on removing variation and smoothing supply. To optimise supply, first set agreements with raw material suppliers then establish agreed lead-times and apply consignment stock, vendor-managed inventory or B2B connections to minimise inventory and risk.

The product streaming concept is based on continuous value-adding, MTO and MTS product classifications. In multi-stage production units, the question is: which products in the early stage should be MTO or MTS? In reality, it will be a mixture of both for multi-product firms, where lead-times for production are greater than the customer expected lead-time. The question is how to decide?

In the case of Dell, with their original model, they simply told the customer what the lead-time was; say, ten days. Originally, they could not supply immediately because they did not carry finished goods at Point of Sale (POS). Lean systems thinking will provide the answers. Such lean programs lead to a revolution in cashflow and the recognition that current accounting systems are inadequate for the improvements required.

With analysis and the overall capability of various activities or machines in a process chain, it is possible to link processes together and therefore have zero inventory and reduce cycle-time between them, provided that Six Sigma quality is achieved. Ideally, the value-added percent should be the same for each process, but variation in production and supply must be minimised by continuous improvement.

The number one rule for continuous flow is matching supply with real demand. Too much inventory erodes profit and often gives rise to quality problems. Too little inventory can lead to a loss of sales that can be accentuated by long lead-times.

4.2 Promotional Variation

In the fast-moving consumer goods (FMCG) industry, fast promotional strategies are used to boost sales. An illustration of such a promotional strategy and its effect on direct sales at a supermarket is shown in Figure 4.4. Dr. Deming would describe this as tampering with the process.

At Week 4, the price was reduced. Sales climbed until there was insufficient stock, which was replenished at Week 8 where sales increased again. The reduction in price did not increase market share as the sales rate returned to its old level when the price was reduced to normal. The above data is the variation in the sales of a common product (high-volume, low-risk MTS) measured at POS and includes a promotional strategy at Week 4. This one was a very simple reduction in price.

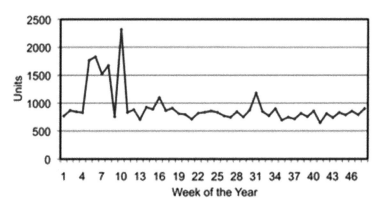

Figure 4.4 Sales promotional at a supermarket – tampered variation.

Note that sales increased and held for a few weeks, but then collapsed before recovering. The supply chain could not cope due to faulty planning. Figure 4.4 represents real demand. It is not necessary to see the detail in these graphs. What we are looking at is the degree of variation. Unfortunately, since there was poor integration between the supermarket and the next upstream process, substantial variation existed upstream and supply could not be maintained. This is a good example of demand amplification.

Figure 4.4 has two main features: a background demand equal to 750 units a day, and a POS promotional strategy at 1,750 to 2,250 over six weeks. Note that the promotional strategy increased sales only temporarily and did not increase market share.

The figure also illustrates the increased variation in the manufacture of the product two stages upstream from the POS due to tampering of the system by not applying lean production rules. This can be avoided with B2B and using the IT lean rules. The whole system must focus on creating a 'pull' system so that a continuous self-perpetuating process is created and maintained. This will require that setups and waste-time are reduced.

The massive variation for monthly production is evident in the figure. If this variation and waste is to be reduced, then we need all the processes in play that support high velocity. The 26 Rules for Lean Systems (see Appendix) are all necessary. Ideally, the product should move continuously and aim for continuous flow. Product and service innovation, and the speed with which new products and services can be introduced to market, can be used as a strategic weapon. Many manufacturers link process and product innovation.

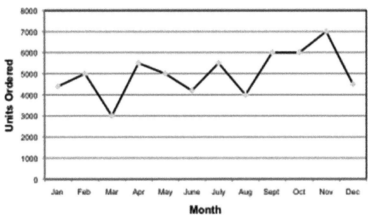

Units Ordered Based on Sales Next Process Downstream

Figure 4.5 Variation – two stages upstream from the point of sale (POS).

It is not advisable to suddenly impose strict rules on the planning and manufacturing processes. Instead, the approach should be to gradually introduce the principles and, if possible, increase the number of MTO lines. MTO lines and reduce the MTS consistent with the delivery requirements of the customers. As well as all the benefits above, lean manufacturing will focus the company on forever improving its quality, manufacturing flexibility, costing systems and response time to customers.

Figure 4.6 is an example of how short lead-times, combined with accurate POS data in real-tie and a 'pull' system operating on a fast, short lead-time, can assist in improving service performance with optimum inventory. This is the model developed for the Speedo-Myer supply chain to calculate minimum inventory holdings. The chances of the retailer in this case having redundant inventory at the end of the season have been minimised. In addition, the possibility of sales being lost due to insufficient POS stock will be minimised.

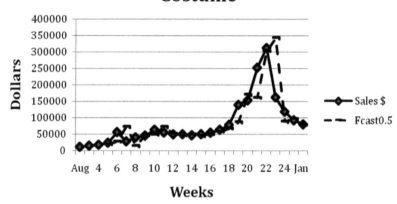

Myer Sales Data Male Swimming Costume

Figure 4.6 Sales of Speedo Swimming Costumes.

The theoretical forecast shown by the dashed line is used to calculate inventory levels needed to ensure no loss of sales and uses the lead-time to Myer as a primary input. The enormous variation in sales is evident.

For most steps in the supply chain, we can link or 'pull' by RPO for high-volume, low-risk products. For high-risk, low-volume products – to minimise waste and loss of profit – we should aim for short lead-times and an intermediate inventory holding point. The longer the forecasting period and the more tampering of the data, the greater the error in supply and the greater the waste.

Lean thinking and its implementation is a journey. The job will not be complete until the lead-time is as close as possible to 100% value-added time and we deliver to our customers the right quality and the right price 100% on-time. This is an impossible target, but the philosophy points the way to continuous improvement.

The answer is velocity with continuous uninterrupted flow, as illustrated in Figure 4.7.

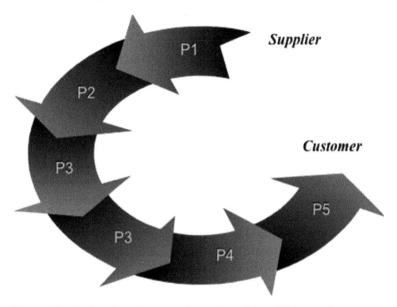

Figure 4.7 The aim of velocity – continuous lean flow at high-speed.

As already emphasised, business is about people, process and precision. Businesses of the future will produce to-demand with small batch sizes and maybe to a batch size of one. Precision of process in all business functions at "Six Sigma" tightness of control creates a strong competitive advantage. Technology and process improvements are advancing at an increasing rate. As a result, new pressures are placed on management and leadership, if they want the enterprise to grow and be competitive. Global supply chains with networks of suppliers feeding strategically placed assembly plants near the market they serve are commonplace, especially in big business.

A key question is how do small businesses, both in manufacturing and service, take advantage of the new and efficient cooperative ways of satisfying customers, with higher expectations, faster than before?

This book offers the solution to this familiar challenge to management ... faster innovation, product and service delivery at a higher-degree of precision ... Six Sigma processes using lean thinking and digital data from the source.

Research requires mental agility. As a result of this – along with the cooperation of over 400 clients both in Australia and overseas and a career dedicated to learning from the best – I have developed 26 rules to analyse and implement lean systems (26 Rules for Lean Systems) and 22 creative ideas to aid innovation of process and product (22 Creative Ideas for Innovation). These have been applied with considerable success, and some of my programs are discussed later.

With the experience of over 900 reports and papers, and numerous innovations and awards by over 400 clients in eight countries, as well as the saving of my own eyesight by applying the 22 Creative Ideas for Innovation described here.

The first three fundamental characteristics of good business practice are quality, cost and delivery aimed at exceeding customer expectations. Add to this innovation and speed with a special focus on continuous improvement. Continuous research and development of both process and product is fundamental. It is clear that to achieve best practice we should have total cooperation in all of the supply chain to achieve maximum benefit for all participants. Cooperating to compete is a strong competitive advantage.

Digital connections to suppliers and customers will assist in making companies more agile. Some innovative companies have clearly demonstrated how the new rules can work very effectively.

With the new digital cooperative lean approach, value-adding by decreasing waste in planning, process and expenses continuously increases as we innovate. Digital connections allow companies to move and use information anywhere along the supply chain. This allows any enterprise in the chain to more accurately forecast or ultimately Make-To-Order (MTO) only.

Such ideas will not work to advantage if the processes are not operating at a high-degree of precision; a level that is now regarded as processes at such a level of reduced variation that the defect rate outside the range of acceptability for the customer is only 3.0 parts per million. Variation in process is a major enemy of speed.

To achieve maximum benefit, the five functions of business – people, operations, marketing and sales, innovation and finance – need to be integrated. This requires the judicious use of people, technology and information, and the continuous training and upgrading of people skills and knowledge. Concentration on the technical aspects of these factors alone will not yield the desired results. The reason is that the most important part of all business is people; whether they are customers, employees, employers or investors. Introducing new technology and techniques is much easier than changing culture and behaviour, but they must go together.

In the early stages of a business transformation, use of simple management tools can lead to significant productivity gains in bottleneck areas of the system, and these can be used as a guide to assist in culture change and further innovations. This is clearly practiced at the plants of Japanese clients I have worked with over the years; companies like Panasonic, Matsushita, Canon, Honda, Toyota and Kawai. Special mention is made in this book of the work of Honda and their BP (Best Position, Productivity, Product, Price, Partners) Program. Honda has a very special place in my heart and mind because of the supremely high-standard of their engine integrity and the fast innovation they apply to linking process and product innovation. They had none of the earlier financial support that Toyota had, and yet have excelled.

When we come to the actual process of changing a bad enterprise into a good one, it is important to realise that you can only go so far in improving culture if all that is changed is the physical environment. If the culture is poor, then physical improvements may result in substantial improvement that can be quickly eroded by a poor Management Team.

This book's core message has developed around 30 years of consulting to management. It takes the latest principles relating to what is commonly called Lean Manufacturing and Total Quality Management (TQM) with the latest management principles, and focuses on compressing supply chains and identifying an improved competitive advantage, the velocity of the processes and systems. Now we can integrate industry 4.0 principles once the basics are in place.

Cross-functionality, innovation and fast financial management within a short time period must be core elements of production and serving customers. The enterprise now must be an integrated structure of people driving innovation to satisfy and exceed customer needs and wants. Measurements of processes and systems must be at the source of the activity, and the financial outcomes must be available quickly. Digital data can satisfy this need. Financial data should be available quickly, but looked upon as real-time output.

It is vital that modern managers understand reporting as well as communication, budgeting and the full implications of profit and loss accounts, balance sheets and cashflow. They must also understand the concept of continuous research and development, training, education, and never-ending improvement. The Board sets the strategy, direction and philosophy that will drive the mindset of managers in the future where innovation, a sharp customer focus, flexibility and speed are urgently needed for all people, processes and systems.

New tools and techniques, such as the 26 Rules for Lean Systems for process improvement and for innovation of process, the 22 Creative Ideas for Innovation will assist management in championing the new approach.

It is the intention of this book to enunciate a new interpretation of the management processes and systems to facilitate a more caring and successful human side to work. This book aims to release the intellect and power of the people and realise the potential of producing to-demand with a batch size of one. It is about high-velocity integrated systems driven by innovative caring management.

Management must learn to:

- Use digital data from the source of the activity and the source of the buying decision more effectively to accelerate and improve the service delivery and product delivered to the customer and end user

- Cope with technical change more successfully

- Understand the philosophy that Australian industry can no longer live with the present levels of productivity, performance, quality and low-level of innovation and lack of research and development

- Plan ahead more effectively, both long-term and short-term
- Take advantage of our natural comparative advantages to create greater employment
- Learn to innovate process and product with greater speed and precision
- Introduce a new approach into Australian companies: there are a number of issues that must be confronted:
  - A decision based on financial accounts alone. What about the manufacturing process? The marketplace should drive the process through manufacturing.
  - Inadequate planning
  - Failure of management to get involved on the shop-floor and understand the real meaning of high-quality at Six Sigma levels and innovation
  - Failure to analyse productivity data and use the scientific method to isolate reasons and eliminate causes of problems
  - A tendency to always blame the worker on the job when most often the process is at fault – this is management's responsibility
  - The removal of lines in demarcation (necessary to improve efficiency), the need for restructuring the workforce and using multi-skilling to a greater degree
  - Poor communication between management and worker
  - Inadequate skills and training at all levels
  - Lack of industrial engineering expertise and operations research

Japanese managers do not make hurried decisions like Australian managers do. They are painstaking in their demands for a cause and effect scientific analysis, and hence require many technical details before they make a decision and a project gets approved. Once the decision is made, however, everyone concerned is convinced it is correct and committed to it. Therefore, they all work to a common goal. Additionally, Japanese people set themselves exceptionally high standards, and this aids in motivation. Consequently, the worker more closely achieves peak performance. Japanese management is efficient and integrated. The emphasis is on consensus in decision-making.

Japanese workers were not always this way. The change began in the USA in 1946 when General MacArthur found the quality of Japanese equipment was very poor. Traditional quality control was introduced, new statistical quality control followed, and a quality revolution resulted. The fathers of this revolution were:

- Dr. Walter A. Shewhart
- Dr. W. Edwards Deming
- Dr. J.M. Juran

These three were all basically ignored in their own country (USA), but their work was revered in Japan. The western world needs to listen to the new philosophy. The way Japan uses people, technology, work organisation; the way Japan improves its process, quality and productivity; the way the workforce is educated and the way they organise themselves is significantly different from the way we do things in western society. In the future, we should take more notice of the way our Asian neighbours work. They cooperate internally and externally much more seamlessly than we do. This cooperation is based upon and directed towards the achievement of a national objective of full employment and a happy, cooperative, fulfilling life for all.

I think the message here is quite plain. We must identify our strategic direction and work together as a team if we are going to be successful in achieving a growth rate that is comparable with countries like Japan, South Korea and Taiwan. We must identify our natural competitive advantages and capitalise on them to succeed, there has to be an increasing emphasis placed on policies that strengthen links between small and large businesses to enhance import substitution. This can be done by encouraging domestic manufacturers to make aluminium components. After all, aluminium with a specific gravity of 2.7 is far less dense and hence lighter than steel at 7.8. The problem is that aluminium is expensive. It requires so much electricity to produce that people often call it solid electricity. Research and development must be viewed as crucial for success. Again, the approach of foreign investment must be balanced, and specific policies directed towards ensuring the maximum benefit to the domestic economy that accrues from both incoming and outgoing investment.

Australia must learn from global experiences and advanced high-velocity cooperative systems similar to those used by, say, ZARA International for women's and men's clothing. ZARA International design in Spain digitally, use a multitude of manufacturers in places like Mauritius, Peru, Thailand and India – in fact, anywhere the labour is cheap – and link directly with the stores that hold only sufficient stock to display and sell over a few days. These stocks are replaced on balanced delivery frequencies. They utilise a digital network more effectively than any other garment manufacturer.

This is a similar system to the one I designed for an Australian yachting supply company. In this case, velocity is used as a competitive advantage, since rapid supply means low-working capital tied up in inventory, storage, rapid setup changes, and synchronised arrivals of finished goods.

For a successful application the industry 4.0 elements need a solid Lean framework in which to operate.

At first glance the explosion of knowledge and opportunities presented by continuous acceleration of new knowledge and the exponential waves of new opportunities this creates appears to be overwhelming. However, once you have devised a strategy and have a framework in place to grow the business further, the introduction of the new ideas becomes much easier.

We must plan for agility. his strategy must fall within an agile framework. The most successful framework within which these new ideas will prosper is one based on the Lean thinking philosophy.

Many people have summarised the Kaizen philosophy as small incremental improvements but Kaizen can lead to massive step function change.

A good example of this thinking was on display when I visited the Canon plant in Toride, Japan, in 2007. Canon were developing a new printing press which became known as the Omnipress. Much of the first stages of commercialisation and the usage of this unique machine was done in Sydney at North Ryde. The philosophy of this was to produced books in the smallest batch size as possible, in fact in a batch size of one. I was fortunate to work with the team in Sydney and we did in fact produce my book "Velocity" in a batch size of one. Inventory could be almost eliminated. The idea was to produce the multi covered covers printed in advance but have the text on a disc or pen-drive and simply have the covers in a tray linked to the machine, press a button and the whole book would be printed and bound with the cover on in the space of a few minutes. This is a good example of how the industry 4.0 concept of digital printing and supply chain compression can save space and money.

I imagined that in the future we could walk into a bookstore and see the book of our choicer but then wait a few minutes while the vendor printed and bound a copy from the Omnipress. So far the machine has only found use in the wholesale area not the retail arena.

Modern businesses must take advantage of the opportunities offered by the appropriate industry 4.0 element to improve and further develop their competitiveness. All these developments must take place within the framework of a good lean structure harnessing the best of the Toyota human approach and the Honda highly mechanised approach.

Internet of Things (IoT). Toyota and Honda advanced the Lean approach in slightly different ways but both produced products of very high quality.

If we move around the centre, we can see that it covers the connections and sharing of data and information covering elements of health, mechanics, music, transport, time, data, communication, mobility, ... in fact anything that can be connected via a sensor or software. IoT has led to an explosion of opportunities. It is limited only by human imagination (see Bibliography).

Many of us are well aware of the explosion in the use of sensors in the modern motor car. Sensors detecting nearness to objects on mudguards and fenders but positioned all around the car to make it safer for pedestrians and other drivers as well as the driver. Collision avoidance technology is now common in the latest vehicles as is sensors to steer the car on a safe path on highways. Similarly, RFID technologies can be used to speed up processes.

Use of On-line Platforms

The usage of on-line Internet platforms like Zoom, Teams and Skype are becoming widespread. These are wonderful tools for peer-to-peer learning despite some inherent disadvantages.

Listening to Customers

Listening to customers has often been called the voice of the customer. If we fail to listen then we are heading for failure. The use of digital platforms has led to a revolution in the way businesses are interacting with customers. A good example of the way businesses are interacting in the value chain and the changes that this makes are better illustrated by the new Agency concept for selling cars being implemented by Honda. The further you are away from the source, the customer the more distorted the message. Honda have recognised that the dealer network is insulating them from the true voice of the customer so they have responded with a new model. Mercedes are also adopting this new model. As expected it is causing a great deal of heartache for the dealers who could now be regarded as largely irrelevant.

Dealers can no longer set the price to the customer. This is set by Honda and no discounts are allowed. Previously Dealers were often bidding against themselves for sales. This will disappear with Agency model. In addition, the capital invested in the real estate of the dealerships will be reduced and much of the customer education and model knowledge will be promulgated over the Internet. This releases more money for research and development. Warranties will be more tightly controlled as will the training and development of the service personnel. All this should mean greater customer satisfaction. Since the Agency relationship will be controlled by Honda the sharing of information between agencies and Honda should improve, The result should be faster customer feedback and solution to problems or speedier further innovation. It will be interesting to see how German companies in particular respond and what this will do to brand capital. In all, cases this concept should help bridge the IT gap between the customer and the factory floor ... always a pet grievance of mine where the person I had to deal with after my car was serviced could not adequately answer my questions. With the introduction of the Agency system the dealer I was using to service my car lost his dealership and I was forced to do to another and suddenly I discovered that the first dealer was not doing all the service work correctly. With the new Agency model this should not happen. As well there will be a greater personalisation of supply.

Cloud computing is on demand availability of computer system resources especially data storage and computer power and knowledge sources. It is a data centre available over the Internet and operates in real time and is available on demand.

Data Analytics and Big Data

The ability to collect data digitally and at light speed enables huge amount of data to be collected to assist in solving problems.

A good example of the use of big data is the collection of multi-spot measurements on the cervix of a woman patient using a sensitive scanning device and immediately feeding this to data base for thousands of women and hen instantaneously assessing whether she has cervical cancer or not. In this case during the setup stage for the device machine learning algorithms based on Bayes Law were used to refine the measuring tool sensitivity.

Another example is the use of the analysis of big data to predict stock market trends. Literally tens of thousands of stocks can be analysed in real time for a large number of parameters such as market cap, div yield, P/E, Peer position, weighted mean average, and many other parameters.

Immediate Everyday Results of the Current Use of Industry 4.0 Concepts

Innovation on Display

There is no better arena for studying rapid innovation than Formula 1 for cars and Moto GP for motorcycles.

The modern F1 car is an example of the latest thinking in moving a powered vehicle at high speed with maximum safety. It places tremendous strain on the Driver and the Pitt crew.

Engine technology continues to evolve with turbo charging, energy savings devices and new ways of controlling the flow of air around the vehicle. The innovation never stops.

The continuous improvement flows into the every-day motor vehicle as most of the significant advances were made I the F1 arena.

The following will serve as examples of rapid innovation.

Red Bull Honda 2021

A good example of how one innovation can lead to many other innovations is well illustrated by the following series of developments.

The Honda engine in the Red Bull is HCC I, i.e. Homogeneous Charge Compression Ignition. It therefore critically important all aspects of the combustion process are under tight control. F1 is about looking for more speed and efficiency continuously. Their latest innovation led to a substantial comparative advantage compared with their main rival, Mercedes. The sequence of innovations is listed below:

1. Honda applied the Kumamoto coating to the walls of the cylinders to decrease friction. This innovation was a direct result of the work done by the Motorcycle Division. There was a drop in temperature as a result of this.
2. This enabled Honda to move the cylinders closer together.
3. This meant the size and weight of the engine block decreased and the heat and recovery systems could be improved. These were improved with help of the HondaJet division.
4. All the above meant that the centre of gravity was lowered.
5. This in turn led to the backend of the chassis being lowered.
6. As a result of this, the rear fin was redesigned and the car we believe had less drag and better downforce control.

The Red Bull Honda is now the fastest F1 car on the circuit.

However, in the rapidly innovative arena of F1 each manufacturer jumps over the other repeatedly. Mercedes will respond but the edge given to Red Bull will probably result in Verstappen becoming the F1 champion in 2021 and Red Bull Honda winning the manufacturers title.

The rapid use of sensors and digital information combined with the high precision of manufactured parts to Six Sigma standards, and the use of algorithms with machine learning accelerated the development and application of these innovations.

It worth noting, as well, the cooperative effort of the 3 Honda divisions in achieving their goal.

I am privileged to have worked with excellent people like Dr. Ezzelino Leonardi of Pirelli, Dr. Bob Blake of Precision Valve Inc, Dr. Chris Roberts of Cochlear, and earlier in my career, Professor Eric Hall, who provided much support and encouragement.

An example of lack of communication and poor management systems was clearly illustrated by one program where management were receiving data indicating that their machines were over 97% efficient. Upon examination it was found that:

- Approximately 50% of all the cavities in the multi cavity injection process were not producing nylon valves but the machine was still doing work as if it was producing twice as many plastic valves per cycle. This was not measured.
- A new method of measurement was implemented which effectively designated the blocked off cavity as a defect.
- The measured defectives of the process, not the product, increased from 15% to 45%. A further analysis revealed the possibility that the causes of the damaged cavities could be eliminated and the overall quality improved with improved process control. The quality department was moved to the shop-floor and the operators were trained and the damaged cavities repaired.
- 40 weeks later, the defect rate was almost zero and the productivity had doubled and it was no longer necessary to buy 14 new injection moulding machines.
- It is useful to record the achievement under our thesis, of people, process and precision.

This is only one of many examples where poor management systems can mislead management.

Chapter 5

Aims of Industry 4.0 and the Lean Framework

Summary

The lean framework is essential if the true benefits of the opportunities offered by the tools of industry 4.0 are to be realised. Globalisation increased the need to be more innovative and clever. The tools of industry 4.0 will enhance competitiveness. To quality, cost and delivery, the cornerstones of successful business, we must add velocity. Companies with the correct use of all the management tools and techniques available can become more agile and respond to changing market needs more quickly. The tools of industry 4.0 are focussed on making the business more profitable and successful. As the full benefits of the improvements take hold, opportunities to further enhance the business by innovating new methods and developing new products and processes will become clearer. The path to improvement never ends.

5.1 Lean Thinking

The application of lean principles to manufacturing plants making a small range of products on long-runs is relatively simple. More difficult is applying these principles to a plant making a large product range on the short runs required to minimise

Technology for Business: Application of the Advances in Industry 4.0 to Small to Medium Sized Enterprises
John Blakemore
Copyright © 2023 Jenny Stanford Publishing Pte. Ltd.
ISBN 978-981-4968-70-6 (Hardcover), 978-1-003-38216-4 (eBook)
www.jennystanford.com

working capital tied up as inventory. This has been discussed in detail in my Australian Graduate School of Engineering Innovation paper – "Maximising Profitability with Short Production Runs" – which is used for training by the United States Air Force. The logic summarised in my paper has been applied many times very successfully. This success is also firmly dependent on the human psychology of its application and implementation.

Akerlof and Shiller in "Animal Spirits" (see bibliography), describing how human psychology drives decision-making, were certainly right. While their work concentrated on how animal spirits drive the world economy and – in particular, market demand – it is clear that the application of their ideas is much broader. One questions Adam Smith's invisible hand of control in his publication "An Inquiry into the Nature and Causes of the Wealth of Nations". Just as economists are split between the rationalists and those postulating that control lies with human behaviour, similar reasoning can be applied to the application of lean thinking principles.

Japanese behaviour lends itself to the rules of high-quality processes, systems and behaviour and a completely different perspective on the way they treat their own people and the way they treat non-Japanese people, but this is changing. Witness a Samurai Warrior and the precision of his movements and the way the Japanese treat terrorist threats. In western society, leaders to do not kowtow to terrorist demands; in Japan, they do, since the lives of their people are sacred. The culture is very different. All Japanese are part of the same team. All members are important.

This has been well-documented in studies published by the Nomura School when I studied there in 1985. The adaptation of strict, highly disciplined rules of behaviour and control as specified using statistical techniques by Dr. Deming, were relatively easy for the Japanese. The application of the lean thinking rules that I have observed in Japanese factories (documented in this book) need to be modified to suit western society culture. When this is done, the rewards flow just as well as that experienced by the Japanese.

When Honda and Toyota first decided to build cars in the most competitive market in the world – the USA – during the early

70s, they quickly demonstrated that cultural difficulties could be overcome. This was despite the fact that the general anti-Japanese car feelings were so high that many Hondas and Toyotas were trashed by unionists in the Ford and General Motors carparks.

Lean thinking is spreading, and the next step is to refine the system to increase the velocity of the value chain. From individual machines and processes to supply chains, all industries are beginning to apply the principles of lean manufacturing and lean thinking to internal and external systems. In addition, Dr. Chris Roberts, CEO of Cochlear – an organisation which is regarded by many as Australia's most innovative company – has described to me in detail how these processes are starting to gain traction in US hospitals for the surgical procedures required to fit the cochlear implant.

The objective of lean thinking principles is to speed up supply, improve reliability, employ less working capital and operate Six Sigma processes. (For the purpose of this book, Six Sigma is defined as per the original Motorola University definition and allows for a 1.5 Sigma shift in the target – this leads to a defect rate of 3.4 parts per million.) Lean thinking will fail if the fundamentals of quality, as described by Dr. Deming, are not practised ... hence my usage of the word precision. This means that the variation has to be reduced so that out-of-specification products or processes are parts per billion, not million, if possible.

This is fundamental if we are to pursue a Make-to-Order (MTO) philosophy. Simply put, if there are four steps, say, and they are integrated with no inventory buffer between them in a series production system then the efficiency of the latest process is a product of the efficiencies of the former three processes. This can be designed into the system by having a greater capability of the processes downstream or by using buffers, but both of these options are expensive and do not address the real problem. To achieve MTO, machinery and labour will need to be precise, operate at high-quality and be highly flexible. This is not always easy because machines often produce at different rates. In general, the application of these principles in a large plant, supplying a product to the global market and producing on long-runs – such as those operating in the USA or Japan – is a formidable task. However, the problems are even more difficult in small companies where plants operate on shorter-runs with greater product variety.

Often in Australia, the machines are not dedicated to one type of operation as they are in, say, Japan where the flexibility is supplied by highly flexible modular machines with off-line setups. The greater complexity of product and process in countries like Australia, for example, is partially a result of its small population, a small local market and its geographical isolation.

In the Auto Industry, it is common for the plants supplying Toyota with components to operate two shifts, five days a week, with 2 hour break between shifts, while making a small range of products. The break is for preventative maintenance and scheduled production shortfall in the previous shift. No doubt Toyota plans to remove this break. To achieve maximum velocity, the value-added time as a percentage of the cycle-time must increase.

The question arises: what is value-added? The best way to look at this is that the only value-added step in a process or system is the part that actually does what it is supposed to do in terms of delivering a product or service, since the major capital investment is in the machinery. Off-line setups become desirable, so that the main asset is producing as continuously as possible. Cleanups, therefore, should occur as the product is being produced. The main process must shut down for maintenance. Processes and systems must operate at a level of quality and reliability such that every part or person replacement is planned for. For this case, the planned preventative maintenance program – where the process is shut down – must be regarded as adding value.

The world-wide study of the Auto Industry – The IMVP, as reported in "The Machine That Changed The World" – has shown benefits of the Toyota production system, the Honda Best Product and lean thinking. This system was born in the Japanese Manufacturing Industry, and flourished because of the Japanese Samurai Warrior culture of perfection, which Dr. Deming was able to capitalise on. It has now spread to hospitals, as described to me by one of my clients – Dr. Chris Roberts for the installation of the Cochlear Implant – but the Health Care Industry has a lot more to do.

The IMVP study showed that the work in process in US manufacturing plants was a thousand times greater than Japanese plants. The Japanese plants were lean. My independent studies in Japan, Germany, France, Australia and Italy, in particular, have verified this concept. In addition, I have also observed that Honda in Sayama near Osaka, where I spent some time, has synchronised body press shops and assembly lines so that they are not restricted to assembling only one make of a car at a time on the same production line. In some plants trying to start at this point there have been difficulties.

The way to go is to continuously reduce the batch size using Kaizen, as described by Imai. Kaizen can best be described as small, incremental improvements which, when practised, often enable people to take a massive step in innovation. This is a direct result of operating lean systems. However, the application of such principles must be backed up by a clear strategy and continuous innovation in product and process. All this is meaningless unless it is supported and practised by people through a supportive, flexible, team-based culture. It requires that staff and employees have a continuously supportive and improving cultural environment. Of course, no one has a mortgage on ideas. Artful workforces harness their creativity through focused teamwork. All businesses must learn to do this so that the human effort is synergised.

In lean systems thinking applied to manufacturing, businesses concentrate on high-quality, maximum value-added, minimum waste, minimum working capital, short lead-times and continuous improvement by innovation and Kaizen. These principles can be directly applied to any industry. (In the Health Care Industry, the rewards will be significant.) Unfortunately, accounting methods still often stifle business creativity because they aim to satisfy taxation and shareholder requirements using financial data usually collected after the event. To maximise velocity, we need data as close to real-time as we can.

Another serious limitation arises in many companies because of the poor connection between marketing and manufacturing, and the lack of understanding of how forecasts on long lead-times work and how errors increase as the lead-time for implementation of the plan increases. There has to be a strategy to continuously reduce the lead-time in all its forms, and this means organisations must focus on increasing the value-added time in all processes and systems.

Conventional accounting methods, especially using standard costs, are usually structured in a way that accurately measure waste, value-added and the correct overhead allocation is lost. Some information technology systems offer an opportunity to help rectify this but, because they are not fully understood by users, many of their competitive advantages are lost.

5.2   Lean Systems

Manufacturing techniques in many plants Making-to-Stock (MTS) have historically worked on forecast data with a six-to-eight week manufacturing plan. Such plans will always be in error. The further organisations extrapolate out into the future, the greater the error will be. These forecasts are trying to satisfy the basic rule of making only what you can sell, but the errors in a mass-production plant with machines and equipment with poor flexibility can lead to over-production, high inventory and high obsolescence. These problems, too, can be overcome with the application of lean system thinking. Often, however, Marketing Departments insist that the finished product must be in stock otherwise they cannot sell it. A new approach is needed.

Lean systems thinking was developed for manufacturing by Toyota when it decided to build cars. Toyota sent Taiichi Ohno around the world to study mass-production techniques first developed by Ford. When Ohno returned, he proposed that Toyota manufacture cars like the US run their supermarkets. This idea was supported by Toyota and the lean system was born: American mass-production was rejected. Indeed, Ohno only had to look as far as the Tokyo sushi bars to see the principle at work. He did not need to visit an American supermarket.

The Toyota System follows a series a logical shop-floor controlled rules with Kanban loops. A Kanban is an instruction to make a batch that arrives at the next process just in time to phase directly in to the machine or process. The inventory between processes is therefore reduced to almost zero, and the batch quantity can be balanced against frequency of delivery. It is easy to see why component suppliers would prefer to be close to the main customer and, when directly digitally linked, monitor production at both ends. This system will work no matter where in the world the supplier may be. To achieve this with minimum inventory buffers, the processes must operate at a higher degree of perfection. We say they must be Six Sigma processes.

Soichiro Honda would not accept any variation at all in theory. Perhaps this is why their motors are bullet-proof. He always wanted perfection. This perfection resulted in outstanding Formula 1 success when teamed up with Ayrton Senna between 1988 and 1992. Senna was killed at Imola in 1994. The photo below shows Ayrton Senna on the left with Soichiro Honda and Alain Prost, circa 1992. This photograph is reprinted with the permission of Honda Australia.

The outstanding perfection in motor precision was built to the Senna-designed Honda NSX illustrated in the photo below:

The Honda NSX was a sensation when first released. When compared with the Ferrari 348 and the Porsche 911, Britain's Autocar scored the NSX five stars to Porsche four stars and the Ferrari three stars. Car Australia reached the same verdict. This wonderful quality was built in to the Honda NSX which, despite its obvious superiority, did not sell well against its rivals.

This shows the value of branding, marketing and what is termed animal spirits. The Ferrari had a long pedigree in racing, and Honda's image was one of a good company building motor cycles and very good small cars. Ferrari was still the preferred vehicle, even though its reliability was questionable. These buying decisions are not rational, but are guided by human emotion. Ferrari did, however, see the light and hired Honda engineers like Osamu Goto to improve processes, and the resulting Formula 1 success of Michael Schumacher became legendary.

Business is certainly a complex organism where the human psychology can drive success. Clearly branding and marketing and stories of celebrity users are paramount in this equation. The idea is to make the manufacturing system as flexible as possible, and run with synchronised processes and maximum value-added with minimum inventory. This means that setup times must approach zero lost time.

The basic aim of lean manufacturing is to introduce a 'pull' system with a short lead-time. The lead-time is made up of two main components: value-added and non-value added time. Value-added time is run time on a machine, for example. Non-value added time is storage time, setup time, idle time, breakdowns and inspection time, for example. An ideal goal is to achieve 100% value-added time. This is practically impossible, of course. But for many plants, the value for the total plant is probably 2% (limited measurements), so the opportunity is very significant. In private conversation with Toyota, they believe they are probably less than 10%. It is a measurement worth taking.

A lean manufacturing system will not work if the manufacturing processes and the machinery do not perform to their statistical capability. Here, the capability is defined in terms of the ratio of the difference in specification limits and usually Three Sigma variation limits, such that if these are equal then the system capability is one. The variation difference at plus or minus. Three Sigma is for a defect rate of 0.3% or 99.7% good. Immediately, we see that this is not good enough, and it was from continuous improvement that plus or minus Six Sigma became a goal. It also means that if the process is operating at Six Sigma, then the capability is many times greater. This is described in detail by Jack ReVelle in "Manufacturing Handbook of Best Practices."

5.3   Globalisation

Globalisation has increased the fierceness of competition. Digitisation will allow us to move data instantaneously to any part of the globe. New manufacturing concepts like those employed by the women's wear and men's wear manufacturer ZARA International, operating from Spain, can be born and take advantage of digital outsourcing of raw materials sent directly to converters who are digitally linked to sales outlets. While it is not possible to move matter or products at digital speed, Kanban loops can still operate inside the IT system and digital information can allow accurate control of inventory and customer service.

As companies grow, they also continuously demand a greater return on capital. The value of the company is largely determined by its cashflow potential measured as a return on its capital investment. Its ability to generate cash will also determine the likelihood of further capital investment to aid further growth.

Lean thinking greatly assists a company to manage its cash more effectively and so avoid the problems that often beset companies if there is a sudden chaotic input, since many do not have the cash reserves available. This is another reason why tying up capital in inventory is not a good idea, and the future should be about trying to make everything to-order, Dell who assemble-to-order like one of my clients, are a good example of this. This will only work if the quality of the components is high and provided that you do not lose control of the quality of the sub-contractors and component suppliers as it appears Dell has done. Inventory not only ties up capital, but also space. It also adds to risk and product obsolescence. The way forward is to reduce the length of the supply chain, if possible, and increase the added value by using the 26 Rules for Lean Systems and so increase the speed of the system ... velocity.

All companies can win by being more skilful and flexible in tapping the full creativity of their people and applying the rules of lean thinking to all processes and systems, and concentrating on quality and speed by eliminating non-value added steps from all processes and systems.

5.4 Rules Assisting Lean Implementation

Over the last 30 years of consulting to a wide range of Manufacturing and Service Industries, and a long period in research and development, I have developed a series of tools to assist management and staff. The first of these is the 26 Rules for Lean Systems and the second is the 22 Creative Ideas for Innovation of process and product.

Make-To-Stock (MTS) is a 'push' system. 'Push' systems were dedicated in the past to long-runs with the ability to satisfy a range of orders by holding inventory at many stages of production. Therefore, they operate with high inventory levels, particularly if the product range is wide. The 'pull' system is a MTO system that puts the emphasis on only producing what is sold and producing in ever-decreasing response times until the value-added time as a percent reaches levels as close as possible to the lead-time. Focus is on decreasing the lead-time. The amount of stock in the system is determined by the product range complexity and the time requirements of the customers.

All plants would claim that they only produce what is required. However, if this is produced on forecast, the further out the extrapolation, the larger this error will be. With a 'pull' system, these errors can be minimised because the validity of the data on which the decisions are based is improved greatly. This is a basic rule of good stock and manufacturing control. It also means not interrupting the plan. This plan should operate on a short cycle-time. This also enables the company to link processes and systems and operate financial systems that more accurately measure cashflow in real-time. Many of the principles by Goldman et al in "Cooperate to Compete" as well as "Agile Competitors and Virtual Organisations" can be realised.

For anyone who has visited German and Japanese plants making similar products, it is clear that the make-inspect-rework philosophy of many of the German plants I witnessed in the 80s and 90s is far inferior and more costly than the preventative philosophy of Japanese plants: monitor-as-you-make with processes possessing a high-degree of statistical capability. The German plants are rapidly changing, despite some protestations by many people particularly in Europe as discussed during an AGSEI Seminar in Sydney in 2000. Some are rapidly changing (Porsche, Audi), while others have already benefited from improvements as a result of the application of lean systems (Ferrari, Harley-Davidson).

Ridding the process of variation by first eliminating the special causes and then addressing the common causes is basic to the success of lean thinking, according to Dr. Deming. Variation is a waste. The increase in variation upstream of the real demand for consumer-based products is illustrated in Figure 5.1. The actual and real variations in demand are both shown. This is for a product or service and is illustrated by the solid line.

The real demand is represented by the bottom-line. This demand amplification was first documented in "Industrial Dynamics" by J. Forrester in 1969.

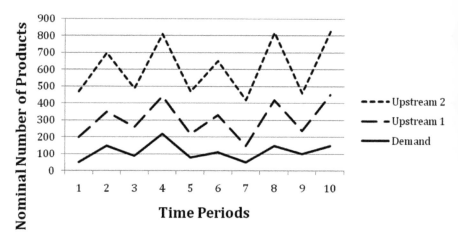

Figure 5.1 Demand amplification over ten time periods.

This model has been prepared from data collected at Coles, Reckitt and Colman and Precision Valve Australia from my own reports. Most of this waste can be removed if accurate digital data on the real demand is fed upstream at high velocity. As we proceed upstream from the customer, the variation increases markedly as shown by the coarse dashed line. One business or process upstream is further amplified as we go further upstream.

This result is called demand process amplification and was first documented by Forrester in his paper "A Major Breakthrough for Decision Makers" and later in his publication "Industrial Dynamics". This variation creates a significant amount of waste and cost.

If the processes operate at a high level of quality and efficiency, then just-in-time delivery can be implemented with a minimum of inventory. The rapid balanced frequency of supply must be matched to-demand as much as possible, but the costs of increased frequency of delivery with smaller batch sizes must be equated to waste, transport costs, working capital, inventory and cashflow.

A simple illustration of the huge negative affect of variation is the effect of feed variation on the quality variation and productivity downstream in a cement factory that I worked in. Minimising the feed variation by buttering the feed in the quarry, tightening the processes of mixing the feed prior to entering the kiln, then not tampering with the process in the kiln itself led to 20-30% productivity gains as the quality improved. This work was done with Gary Lingford and the cement factory teams.

Richard Hammond, the Chief Executive Officer of Adelaide Brighton, appreciated the result and it prolonged the life and jobs in a doomed plant for many years. The tampering with the speed of the kiln was heavily influenced by psychological, non-scientific factors and was a good illustration of how well-meaning and caring operators – well-intentioned as they are – can make matters worse by changing parameters in a process when it is unnecessary.

This can be demonstrated by using the Deming funnel experiment. One director I worked with was continuously tampering with the system and after five years claimed he had improved the forecasting system from an error of plus or minus 50% to plus or minus 45%. With application of lean velocity techniques this error was reduced to less than 5%.

'Pull' systems internally in a plant will lead to inventory points disappearing. Between plants, the duplication of inventory will disappear. This means increasing the run percentage absolutely and as a percent of crewed hours. Hence, setup and cleanup time must be reduced by offline setups, concurrent engineering or special techniques called Single Minute Exchange of Dies (SMED) or techniques using clever tools and jigs as described by Shigeo Shingo in "Shinguru Dandori". Waste in this context is anything not adding value. The speed of the system is set by the bottleneck.

Simply put: aim to 'pull' from an inventory point to the customer point, and work to eliminate the bottleneck using SMED, flexible labour or concurrent engineering. This all means that the value-added time must be maximised as the quality is improved and the processes operate at exceptionally high levels of precision and control (Six Sigma). To achieve this, the process should be split into six parts, as shown in Figure 5.2.

Maximize Value Added

PROCESS PARTS (6)

| 1 | 2 | 3 | 4 | 5 | 6 |

1 - *Setup(Preparation)*
2 - *Run(The Value Added Step)*
3 - *Maintenance (Preventive)*
4 - *Breakdown(Errors & Rework)*
5 - *Idle(available to run but not utilised*
6 - *Cleanup*

Figure 5.2 Six parts of process.

Maximising the value-added part enables the correct quantity to be made consistent with the optimum Economic Production Run (EPR) and the levels of setup, cleanup and sequencing through the plant. The EPR must be continuously reduced after this value is determined from the whole system, not just the process.

The methods of logistical control and movement can be optimised using statistical methods; Statistical Process Control (SPC), as described in detail by Dr. Shewhart, Dr. Deming's mentor, in "Economic Control of Quality of Manufactured Product". The batch size or Equal Batches Every Time (EBET) is often a multiple of the EPR because of logistical considerations. We need, therefore, to measure the EPR for the system. System, here, is defined as the sum of all processes in the value chain. Once again, through animal spirits, the psychological factors identified by Akerlof and Shiller, can be rate-determining.

Examples of the overriding influence of non-rational factors or factors relating to immediate financial reward at the expense of long-term gain influence decision-making to an inordinate degree. Often, rewards offered for total productivity to department managers are in conflict with the best interests of the company.

Nowhere was this better illustrated than at Carter Holt Harvey where the paper-making machines produced more paper than could be used by the next converter processes and, as a result, paper had to be stored offsite. It was moved by forklift along a public road for storage and then brought back again to be converted. Simply reducing the total paper produced reduced working capital by $11 million with a further significant saving in waste, transport, storage and reduced time for the next process. The next step was to reduce the EPR and enable two paper machines to do the work previously completed by three.

The essence of this work was to first determine the correct inventory points and then control them at shop-floor level by replacement. This is aimed at load-levelling and smoothing the load to the optimum by judicious sequencing of products. The objective is to keep the product moving by matching process run times and linking individual machines and processes if possible. It is about continuous flow ... velocity.

Blakemore Consulting International has developed 26 rules to aid in the implementation of lean synchronous systems as summarised in Table 5.1 (see www.blakemore.com.au for more).

These 26 Rules for Lean Systems are grouped into four sub-groups: (1) People, (2) Integration, (3) Planning and (4) Operations. All four groups are important. The order is also the priority of the groups. Not all rules can be applied to all enterprises.

Following Akerof and Shiller, McGregor in "The Human Side of Enterprise", Ouchi's "Theory Z: Japanese Management Practices", and the work of Elton Mayo at the Hawthorne factory in Chicago as discussed by Brown in "The Social Psychology of Industry", it is important to emphasise that the psychology of the workplace is dominant and rationality, while it should always be the driver, often is not. The other psychological issues of great importance are the Zimbardo's "A Pirodellian Prison", "The Hawthorne Effect", the self-fulfilling prophesy, and the grapevine (viz the World War 1 Chinese whisper, "Send reinforcements – we are going to advance", which becomes, "Send me three and fourpence – we are going to a dance").

Table 5.1 26 Rules for Lean Systems

People	
1.	Continuously improve the culture
2.	Team-up
3.	Optimise customer response
Integration	
4.	Supply equals demand
5.	'Pull' for minimum cycle-time
6.	Apply to supply chain
7.	Minimise variation
8.	Shorten the financial cycle
9.	Apply 6S System
Planning	
10.	Demand to bottleneck
11.	Even mix for production
12.	First in first and prioritise
13.	Optimize supply
14.	Load-levelling
15.	Equal batches at the Economic Production Run (EPR)
16.	Optimise sequencing
Operations	
17.	Minimize waste
18.	Aim for continuous flow
19.	Maximise value-added
20.	Link processes
21.	Match processes
22.	Minimise hold points
23.	Prevention not rework
24.	Use Statistical Process Control (SPC) to improve control to Six Sigma
25.	Use Single Minute Exchange of Dies (SMED)
26.	Use quality systems as part of the business processes

All work is influenced by the culture of the workplace and the leadership of the Executive Team. The CEO sets the scene.

Culture, teamwork and customer focus are paramount. The next most important group is the integration of processes and systems. Right at the top of this group is supply equals demand. Only make what the customer wants – MTO – if possible. Of course, if the production make cycle is greater than the customer expected lead-time or promised lead-time then the customer needs to be satisfied from inventory and therefore MTS, but the focus must be on minimising the quantity that is held in inventory to maintain 100% on-time deliveries.

In one program, working capital was reduced by $40 million in 2.7 years, while on-time deliveries improved from 32.7% to 99%, and the finished goods inventory was reduced by $11 million. Anyone can take out working capital and send a company broke. The application of the 26 Rules for Lean Systems companies to take out the capital and make the company more agile and more competitive and profitable. This company then floated, but animal spirits took over. While the company held profitability for two more years, the Chief Executive and Board changed tack and made a completely new product range to stock they could not sell (see www.blakemore.com.au for more). This is discussed in more detail in Chapter 9 and 10. A well-known retail chain did a similar thing many years earlier and almost did not survive.

This was the exact opposite of the system that had moved the company from a loss of $0.5 million to earnings before interest, tax and amortisation of approximately $40 million. How could the Board make such a bad decision? Did greed and irrational exuberance take over? If the company floated, the Chief Executive Officer and Board could become rich. The psychological factors of animal spirits at play here were: confidence (they were over-confident with the success of the rescue and thought they were invincible), fairness (they increased selling prices to the detriment of the customer this was hardly fair at the time), corruption and bad faith (substantial bonuses were paid on the basis of results that they only contributed to in a very minor way) and money illusion (greed). The Marketing Department and the Chief Executive Officer had broken the golden rule: supply equals demand and MTO where possible, and only MTS if you can guarantee it will sell for the right and profitable price.

Soichiro Honda had often said that he created the market, but look what happened to the Honda NSX. Sony, on the other hand, did create a market for the walkman against the best marketing advice available at the time, as described in "Made in Japan: Akio Morita and Sony" by Akio Morita et al. This was the exact opposite to what I had done in the initial rescue operation, so in some cases it will work. In Sony's case, the wrong questions must have been asked in the market survey.

In Table 5.2, we have 6S System. Originally designed as the five pillars of the visual work place as a 5S System, we can add a necessary 6 to this; Safely. The 6S System is a useful place to start lean system introduction. It is purely good housekeeping.

Table 5.2 5S System and 6S System

6S Housekeeping
These are visual tools to improve productivity
1. Sort
2. Set in order
3. Shine
4. Standardise
5. Sustain
6. Safely

The introduction of lean, and then velocity, must be strategic to be successful. Running a successful business is about knowing where to steer the enterprise by defining goals (strategy) and developing the procedures, systems, processes and products to achieve these goals (capability). It is useful to consider the sailing analogy as shown in Figure 5.3.

The yacht is sailing to win by continuously pursuing its goals and improving its competitive position using its assets to greatest advantage. We continuously improve our position by developing and improving products and processes: diligent tiller and sheet trimming; reading the wind tide and waves to best advantage; forecasting changes in the environment. In business, the assets are the people, plant and equipment. Control involves people, plant, processes and systems. Strategic objectives can be achieved by identifying key performance measures and the core processes that lead to the defined and desirable goals. All measurements must be meaningful.

Key Drivers of Business Strategy

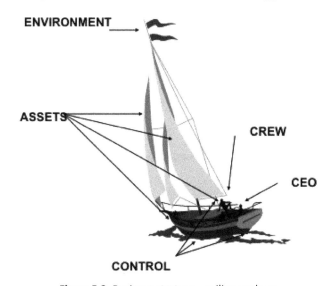

Figure 5.3 Business strategy – sailing analogy.

The overall strategy for improvement must, in the first instance, look at the scheduling and control system for running the company. For a company which has typically made consumer goods to stock, a sales profile for the product range is shown in Figure 5.4.

In Figure 5.4, there are some products that are high-volume, and some that are not (stock keeping units are in '000s). The selling price for slow-moving lines could be increased to recover the extra cost, but this could prove fatal. The gross margin is usually the difference between the selling price and Cost of Goods Sold (COGS). The COGS includes operational costs, but does not include such things as inventory holding costs and obsolescence for the usual case of the profit and loss account for manufacturing companies. This is a massive oversight that can be corrected if the accounting system aims for real-time accounting and is forced to allocate all expenses and costs correctly. The net profit curve includes all costs but, unfortunately, most of the overheads and inefficiencies are aggregated.

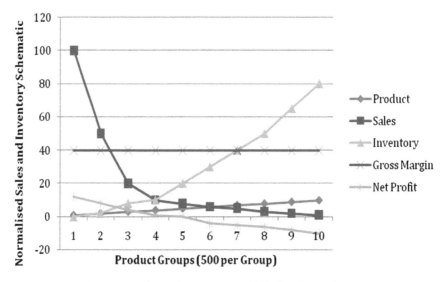

Figure 5.4 Sales and inventory profile before lean velocity.

In Figure 5.4, the company in question believed that it operated the low-volume lines profitably. It is little wonder that with lean the profit suddenly increased from a loss to a substantial profit as the over-production and write-downs disappeared.

In Figure 5.4, the production profile at Stage 1 of a lean introductory program is illustrated once the demand, lead-time and on-time delivery considerations have been determined. When it was explained to the company that Rule 1 of the 26 Rules for Lean Systems was supply must equal demand, Figure 5.5 was drawn up. This figure is based on real data, is not just theoretical and it illustrates the over-production of slow-moving lines. The negative values are the over-stocking due to over-production.

Since the plant was at capacity, it is clear that if they made on-demand the inventory would reduce and the late deliveries of the high-volume lines would disappear and this is exactly what happened. Convincing the CEO and the Marketing Department of this was very difficult. It also meant that the write-downs, which were in excess of $2.5 million per year, disappeared. The company then without consultation, put up prices because it was now delivering on time? Greed took over and customers became upset.

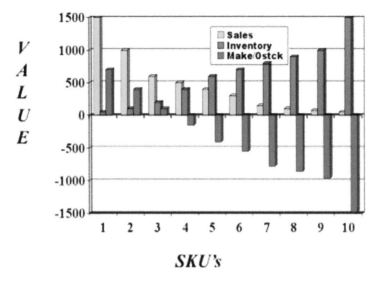

Figure 5.5 Over-production before lean production.

It is very easy to remove inventory and working capital and improve the balance sheet and bankrupt the company. The challenge is to reduce the inventory and improve the on-time deliveries and make more profit. With the 26 Rules for Lean Systems, the on-time deliveries improved as shown in Figure 5.6.

The core measurements in a lean manufacturing system are all related to quality cost and delivery. Lead-times must be reduced to match the expectations of the customers. Ideally, if the exact delivery lead-time to meet the customer's expectation was known, and if the processes to produce in that time were in place, then every product could be MTO with no finished goods inventory. The obsolescence in this system would be zero.

In most companies, this is not feasible. However, for low-risk, high-demand products, some inventory can be held if the production time is greater than that which will satisfy customers. For higher-risk products, where the production lead-time is equal to the sales in that period, we can phase our production to fit the expected demand based on the movements and sales from the previous period. This classification is largely dependent on sales volume, and the EPR for the total process plant and equipment.

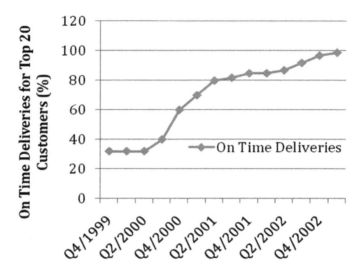

Figure 5.6 On-time deliveries as the inventory was removed.

The EPR is mainly set by the cost of setups, changeovers and cleanups, as shown in Figure 5.7.

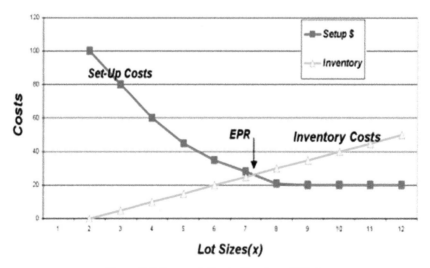

Figure 5.7 Economic Production Runs (EPRs).

The key to reducing the minimum quantity to make and controlling inventory by 'pull' methods is to reduce setups. The EPR for a plant with complex processing routes will be set by the production unit with the lowest value-added time percent, but this is mainly determined by the cost of a setup or changeover compared with the cost to run (add value). In a plant producing a wide variety of products on short runs, as a start, it would be beneficial to isolate the appropriate inventory stage to hold product. In the case of most plants, this will be the point at which there is the greatest increase in the variety of the product. This then becomes the point from which the planning cycle will 'pull' to the customer at an early stage of the introduction of the 'pull' Japanese system.

For the case of one of my clients, this created an opportunity to reduce the variety of intermediate products. From knowledge of the downstream production processes, the new inventory levels were calculated at the intermediate stage and the finished goods stage with the aim of reducing working capital then setting up a system of despatch direct to a distributor from the final production stage.

Chapter 6

Operations Designed to Maximise Value Added

Summary

This chapter adds to the industry 4.0 tools the tools of modern management that are basic to business improvement. Tools like scientific problem solving, and value stream mapping. These tools are often discussed as the quality tools. The aim is to eliminate errors and rework and implement processes that are operating at a high degree of precision. When this is achieved, the business can continue to innovate and further improve its profitability and cash flow. The value-added part of the process and system must be continuously improved.

Business is about people, process and precision. Businesses of the future will produce to-demand with small batch sizes and maybe to a batch size of one. Precision of process in all business functions at "Six Sigma" tightness of control creates a strong competitive advantage. Technology and process improvements are advancing at an increasing rate. As a result, new pressures are placed on management and leadership, if they want the enterprise to grow and be competitive. Global supply chains with networks of suppliers feeding strategically placed assembly plants near the market they serve are commonplace, especially in big business.

Technology for Business: Application of the Advances in Industry 4.0 to Small to Medium Sized Enterprises
John Blakemore
Copyright © 2023 Jenny Stanford Publishing Pte. Ltd.
ISBN 978-981-4968-70-6 (Hardcover), 978-1-003-38216-4 (eBook)
www.jennystanford.com

A key question is how do small businesses, both in manufacturing and service, take advantage of the new and efficient cooperative ways of satisfying customers, with higher expectations, faster than before?

This book offers the solution to this familiar challenge to management ... faster innovation, product and service delivery at a higher-degree of precision ... Six Sigma processes using lean thinking and digital data from the source.

Research requires mental agility. As a result of this – along with the cooperation of over 400 clients both in Australia and overseas and a career dedicated to learning from the best – I have developed 26 rules to analyse and implement lean systems (26 Rules for Lean Systems) and 22 creative ideas to aid innovation of process and product (22 Creative Ideas for Innovation). These have been applied with considerable success, and some of my programs are discussed in Chapter 9.

With the experience of over 900 reports and papers, and numerous innovations and awards by over 400 clients in eight countries, as well as the saving of my own eyesight by applying the 22 Creative Ideas for Innovation described here, I feel confident enough to write this book. I hope all businesses can benefit as my clients have done.

The first three fundamental characteristics of good business practice are quality, cost and delivery aimed at exceeding customer expectations. Add to this innovation and speed with a special focus on continuous improvement. Continuous research and development of both process and product is fundamental. It is clear that to achieve best practice we should have total cooperation in all of the supply chain to achieve maximum benefit for all participants. Cooperating to compete is a strong competitive advantage.

Digital connections to suppliers and customers will assist in making companies more agile. Some innovative companies have clearly demonstrated how the new rules can work very effectively.

With the new digital cooperative lean approach, value-adding by decreasing waste in planning, process and expenses continuously increases as we innovate. Digital connections allow companies to move and use information anywhere along the supply chain. This allows any enterprise in the chain to more accurately forecast or ultimately Make-To-Order (MTO) only.

Such ideas will not work to advantage if the processes are not operating at a high degree of precision; a level that is now regarded as processes at such a level of reduced variation that the defect rate outside the range of acceptability for the customer is only 3.0 parts per million. Variation in process is a major enemy of speed.

To achieve maximum benefit, the five functions of business – people, operations, marketing and sales, innovation and finance – need to be integrated. This requires the judicious use of people, technology and information, and the continuous training and upgrading of people skills and knowledge. Concentration on the technical aspects of these factors alone will not yield the desired results. The reason is that the most important part of all business is people; whether they are customers, employees, employers or investors. Introducing new technology and techniques is much easier than changing culture and behaviour, but they must go together.

In the early stages of a business transformation, use of simple management tools can lead to significant productivity gains in bottleneck areas of the system, and these can be used as a guide to assist in culture change and further innovations. This is clearly practiced at the plants of Japanese clients I have worked with over the years; companies like Panasonic, Matsushita, Canon, Honda, Toyota and Kawai. Special mention is made in this book of the work of Honda and their BP (Best Position, Productivity, Product, Price, Partners) Program. Honda has a very special place in my heart and mind because of the supremely high standard of their engine integrity and the fast innovation they apply to linking process and product innovation. They had none of the earlier financial support that Toyota had, and yet have excelled.

When we come to the actual process of changing a bad enterprise into a good one, it is important to realise that you can only go so far in improving culture if all that is changed is the physical environment. If the culture is poor, then physical improvements may result in substantial improvement that can be quickly eroded by a poor Management Team.

This book's core message has developed around 30 years of consulting to management. It takes the latest principles relating to what is commonly called Lean Manufacturing and Total Quality Management (TQM) with the latest management principles, and focuses on compressing supply chains and identifying an improved competitive advantage, the velocity of the processes and systems.

It is important to understand that the methods described are proven, scientific and logical, but their successful implementation will not work without the support and leadership of a good Management Team. The culture and vision of this team and the company is set by the Chief Executive Officer, Senior Management and the Board. The basic thesis is that western-style management has recognised the superior performance of many Japanese companies, such as Toyota, Honda, Panasonic and Canon, and has attempted to duplicate their formula with (in many cases) a high-degree of failure, particularly for American automotive manufacturers. Why? In almost all cases in the literature, the reason is associated with the people function, leadership and culture, not the technology or technical techniques.

Successful modern management involves a sharp customer focus and the rapid use of high-quality information via digital computer systems that are conveyed through a network of teams in a compressed hierarchical structure. The organisational structure must allow creativity, communication, improvement and innovation of all processes and functions. Companies must plan for the long-term and plans should be continually updated. People must be rewarded for creativity, communication skills and continuous improvement and innovation. The focus is on precision, speed and quality in the entire supply chain.

Cross-functionality, innovation and fast financial management within a short time period must be core elements of production and serving customers. The enterprise now must be an integrated structure of people driving innovation to satisfy and exceed customer needs and wants. Measurements of processes and systems must be at the source of the activity, and the financial outcomes must be available quickly. Digital data can satisfy this need. Financial data should be available quickly, but looked upon as real-time output.

It is vital that modern managers understand reporting as well as communication, budgeting and the full implications of profit and loss accounts, balance sheets and cashflow. They must also understand the concept of continuous research and development, training, education, and never-ending improvement. The Board sets the strategy, direction and philosophy that will drive the mindset of managers in the future where innovation, a sharp customer focus, flexibility and speed are urgently needed for all people, processes and systems.

New tools and techniques, such as the 26 Rules for Lean Systems for process improvement and for innovation of process, the 22 Creative Ideas for Innovation will assist management in championing the new approach.

It is the intention of this book to enunciate a new interpretation of the management processes and systems to facilitate a more caring and successful human side to work. This book aims to release the intellect and power of the people and realise the potential of producing to-demand with a batch size of one. It is about high-velocity integrated systems driven by innovative caring management.

6.1   Fast Future

Management must learn to:

- Use digital data from the source of the activity and the source of the buying decision more effectively to accelerate and improve the service delivery and product delivered to the customer and end user
- Cope with technical change more successfully
- Understand the philosophy that Australian industry can no longer live with the present levels of productivity, performance, quality and low-level of innovation and lack of research and development
- Plan ahead more effectively, both long-term and short-term
- Take advantage of our natural comparative advantages to create greater employment
- Learn to innovate process and product with greater speed and precision

- Introduce a new approach into Australian companies, there are a number of issues that must be confronted:
    - A decision based on financial accounts alone. What about the manufacturing process? The marketplace should drive the process through manufacturing.
    - Inadequate planning
    - Failure of management to get involved on the shop-floor and understand the real meaning of high-quality at Six Sigma levels and innovation
    - Failure to analyse productivity data and use the scientific method to isolate reasons and eliminate causes of problems
    - A tendency to always blame the worker on the job when most often the process is at fault – this is management's responsibility
    - The removal of lines in demarcation (necessary to improve efficiency), the need for restructuring the workforce and using multi-skilling to a greater degree
    - Poor communication between management and worker
    - Inadequate skills and training at all levels
    - Lack of industrial engineering expertise and operations research

Japanese managers do not make hurried decisions like Australian managers do. They are painstaking in their demands for a cause and effect scientific analysis, and hence require many technical details before they make a decision and a project gets approved. Once the decision is made, however, everyone concerned is convinced it is correct and committed to it. Therefore, they all work to a common goal. Additionally, Japanese people set themselves exceptionally high standards, and this aids in motivation. Consequently, the worker more closely achieves peak performance. Japanese management is efficient and integrated. The emphasis is on consensus in decision-making.

Japanese workers were not always this way. The change began in the USA in 1946 when General MacArthur found the quality of Japanese equipment was very poor. Traditional quality control was introduced, new statistical quality control followed, and a quality revolution resulted. The Fathers of this revolution were,

Dr. Walter A. Shewhart, Dr. W. Edwards Deming, and Dr. J.M. Juran. These three pioneers were all basically ignored in their own country (USA), but their work was revered in Japan. The western world needs to listen to the new philosophy. The way Japan uses people, technology, work organisation; the way Japan improves its process, quality and productivity; the way the workforce is educated and the way they organise themselves is significantly different from the way we do things in western society. In the future, we should take more notice of the way our Asian neighbours work. They cooperate internally and externally much more seamlessly than we do. This cooperation is based upon and directed towards the achievement of a national objective of full employment and a happy, cooperative, fulfilling life for all.

I think the message here is quite plain. We must identify our strategic direction and work together as a team if we are going to be successful in achieving a growth rate that is comparable with countries like Japan, South Korea and Taiwan. We must identify our natural competitive advantages and capitalise on them.

To succeed, there has to be an increasing emphasis placed on policies that strengthen links between small and large businesses to enhance import substitution. This can be done by encouraging domestic manufacturers to make aluminium components. After all, aluminium with a specific gravity of 2.7 is far lighter than steel at 7.8. The problem is that aluminium is expensive, solid electricity. Research and development must be viewed as crucial for success. Again, the approach of foreign investment must be balanced, and specific policies directed towards ensuring the maximum benefit to the domestic economy that accrues from both incoming and outgoing investment.

All enterprises must learn from global experiences and advanced high-velocity cooperative systems similar to those used by, say, ZARA International for women's and men's clothing. ZARA International design in Spain digitally, use a multitude of manufacturers in places like Mauritius, Peru, Thailand and India – in fact, anywhere the labour is cheap – and link directly with the stores that hold only sufficient stock to display and sell over a few days. These stocks are replaced on balanced delivery frequencies. They utilise a digital network more effectively than any other garment manufacturer.

This is a similar system to the one I designed for an Australian yachting supply company. In this case, velocity is used as a competitive advantage, since rapid supply means low-working capital tied up in inventory, storage, rapid design changes, and fast-synchronised arrivals of finished clothing at stores and manufacture.

6.2   Process Improvement

To improve global competitiveness, there has to be continuous focus on process and system improvement so that future goals can be achieved, may be exceeded, and competitive advantages continuously honed. To achieve this, enterprises need a strategy and the appropriate tactics. Everything is a process, which can be defined as the conversion of inputs via activities to an output. With miniscule detail, all processes must be improved and innovations introduced utilising the latest technology, knowledge and knowhow. Process improvement can be learned. Unfortunately, much of our education system is geared to teach what to think, not how to think. School teaches knowing; life teaches doing. Our education system, to be more effective, should associate more with doing. It is the same with the implementation of lean high-velocity systems; apply the rules with demonstration pilot projects. If companies are to become successful process improvers, problem-solvers and innovators, they must avoid the:

- Tendency to avoid problems that are not easily solved
- Tendency to attempt only easy problems
- Negative attitudes
- Tendency to be blinkered and not lateral thinkers

Bransford and Stein in "Ideal Problem Solver" (Scientific American Special) use the acronym 'IDEAL' to help:

1. I = Identifying problems
2. D = Defining problems
3. E = Exploring alternatives
4. A = Acting on a plan
5. L = Looking at effects

In his book "New Think", De Bono distinguishes between vertical thinking and lateral thinking. He states:

> Logic is the tool that is used to dig holes deeper and bigger, to make them altogether better holes. But if the hole is in the wrong place, then no amount of improvement is going to put it in the right place. No matter how obvious this may seem to every digger, it is still easier to go on digging in the same place than to start all over again in a new place. Vertical thinking is digging the same hole deeper, lateral thinking is trying again elsewhere.

Einstein had a simpler way of saying this:

> "Logic will lead you from A to B, but imagination will take you anywhere."

6.3   Complex Problems

The Scientific Method utilises the following with an emphasis on experimentation, data collection and logical analysis:

- Experience
- Observation
- Description
- Cause and effect
- Analysis – lateral and vertical thinking
- Synthesis
- Simplification
- Hypothesis (a trial idea)
- Deduction
- Logic
- Experimentation
- Models
- Prediction
- Japanese Gemba Walk (attention, concentration, assimilation, association)

Experience has shown that the following problem-solving flowchart (Figure 6.1) never fails. It uses any of the management and quality tools described next to assist in a team environment to improve processes.

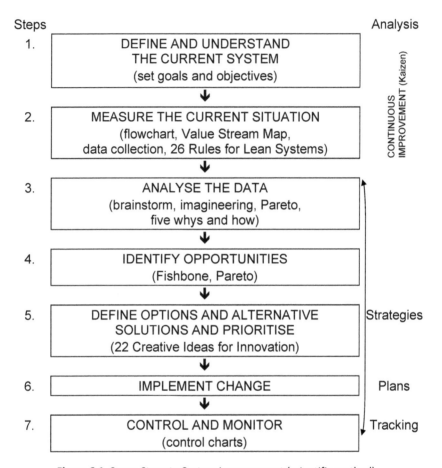

Figure 6.1 Seven Steps to System Improvement (scientific method).

6.4 Management Tools

To assist the transition to a lean high-velocity system, the Japanese use simple management tools, including the seven tools used in Japan under the original banner of Total Quality Control (TQC), then TQM, to assist management and process improvement. These are:

- Brainstorming (team synergy)

- Flowcharts
- Value Stream Map
- Data collection checksheets
- Data types
- Run charts
- Frequency distribution (histogram) and the normal distribution
- Magic lanterns
- Statistics
- Stratification
- Scatter diagrams
- Cause and effect diagrams
- Pareto charts
- Team problem-solving
- Control charts
- Reducing variation to Three Sigma then Six Sigma

6.5   Brainstorming (Team Synergy)

Brainstorming explained in its most basic way, is using a team of people to stimulate the production of ideas. It is almost always more effective than trying to generate ideas alone. The effectiveness of brainstorming in unlocking the creative power of the group (synergy) has long been understood. To start a brainstorming session, ask the members of a group to determine what problems exist in the workplace. It is important to be precise as possible in stating the topic. The definitions should be reasonably specific.

Brainstorming works best when certain rules are followed. The leader should preview these prior to each session. These rules are as follows:

- Each member, in order, is asked for ideas – this continues until all ideas have been exhausted
- Everyone should strive for quantity of ideas to maximise the effectiveness of the team process. Not necessarily quality – no appraisal of ideas occurs yet.
- People offer only one idea per turn
- If a member does not have an idea he/she should say 'pass'

- o No idea is regarded as silly
- o Good natured laughter, informality and exaggeration should be encouraged

Brainstorming begins only after the rules have been explained. The leader will often have to abbreviate a lengthy idea into a few words with the agreement of the originator. During brainstorming no evaluation of suggested ideas should occur. The process will be expedited if a member writes the ideas on butcher's paper as they are given. The second stage is voting on the ideas. The leader records each vote next to the idea. Members can vote for as many ideas as they feel have value. Only supporting votes are taken. Highlight those ideas that received the most votes. Many of the top ideas will be so identified. Now the team can focus on a few important items instead of being somewhat confused by a large number of them.

There are a number of items to keep in mind as the team explores the subject of brainstorming.

- An agenda distributed prior to the meeting will give members a chance to think about the upcoming brainstorming topic and perhaps have several ideas all set to go when the meeting starts
- A large sheet of paper should be used when brainstorming
- Look to nature to creative breakthroughs
- New ideas are generated by thinking big and exaggerating
- Combinations of existing concepts or units may lead to new and exciting creations
- Fantasy can help – an example is to imagine that the laws of gravity can be cancelled. Perhaps something like that happened when the Great Wall of China was conceived or the Pyramids of Egypt were built; that is, create a mind picture.
- The pursuit of concepts during brainstorming may lead to new and sometimes superior products that often cost less
- Incubation often occurs after the initial brainstorming session. 'Let's sleep on it' is a frequently voiced comment. Later, many innovative ideas may emerge.

Brainstorming Summary

- Thought-generating session
- Ideas flow freely
- No appraisal occurs
- Variations encouraged

An alternative method, called Imagineering, is also helpful:

- Listing ideals
- Listing actuals
- Noting differences
- Ranking differences

An opinion-based setting priorities follows. In manufacturing, for example, we may construct a model of our ideal manufacturing plant and strive to move the real plant as close to this ideal model as is practicable.

6.6 Flowcharts

As part of the identifying and defining of the process and problem, it is useful and necessary to flowchart the process and problem so that the members can understand the purpose and objectives of the improvement process. Flowcharts take two forms: standard charts using symbols and Value Stream Maps using the symbols in the Appendix. Flowcharts offer the advantages that:

- Make complex structures and inter-relationships more easily understood with a visual chart (83% of all information is transmitted through sight)
- Help break the problem into smaller parts
- Give more information on a page – 'within eye's reach'

Value Stream Maps offer the extra advantage in that they include data boxes that record the measurements of the rate of flow and production. All symbols are all described in detail in Appendix 1.

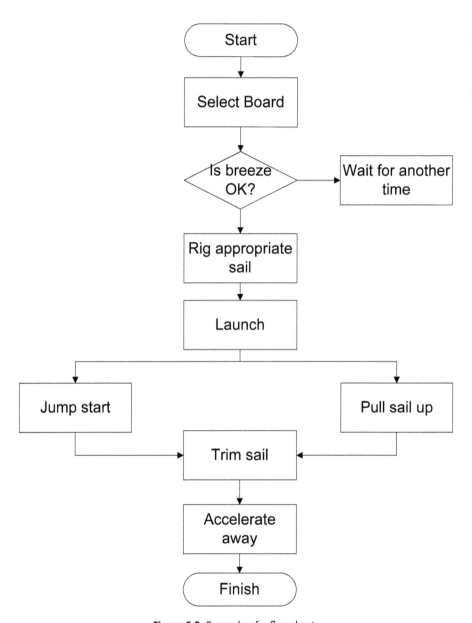

Figure 6.2 Example of a flowchart.

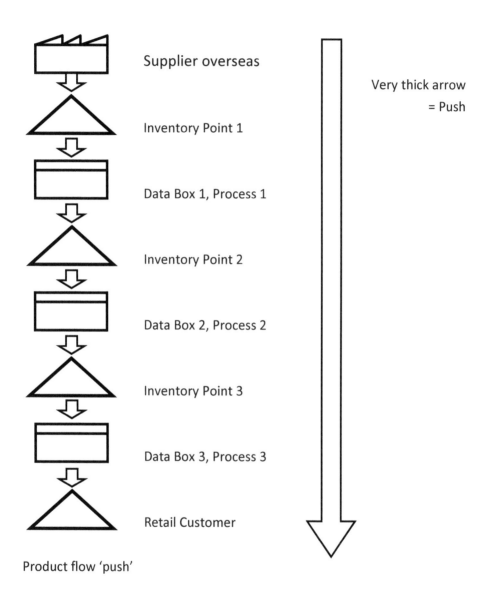

Figure 6.3 Example of a Value Stream Map before lean velocity.

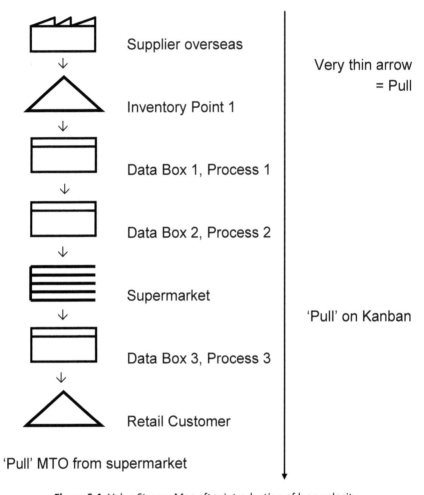

Figure 6.4 Value Stream Map after introduction of lean velocity.

6.7 Data Collection Checksheets

Data is information. After we have decided what the project is and defined its objectives, we must decide on what data we need to collect. The data must be reliable, representative and reproducible.

The five reasons to collect data are:

1. Data for analysis

This is the collection of data to aid in establishing a cause – from this, a relationship can be established between a defect and the reasons why it is defective

2. Data for process control

   The aim here is to monitor the performance and ensure the process remains ideal

3. Data to assist our understanding of the process

   This is raw information collected in the early stage of a process improvement study. Examples are:

   - Number of customer complaints received per day
   - Percentage of defectives produced per day
   - Range of items processed per day
   - The dispersion of part dimensions or properties (hardness, strength, ductility, etc.)

4. Data for regulation

   Data needed to correct deviations

5. Acceptance or rejection data

   Sampling plans as per international standards or military standards like MILSTD 105D should be used.

Data Types

There are three basic data types:

- Measurement data
- Countable data
- Data in relative merits or grade points

Examples of measurement data would be:

- Gauge of aluminium foil
- Weight of patient in a hospital
- Speed of cars along highway

Examples of countable data are:

- Number of defective garments in a shipment
- Number of pin holes in a coated petrol tank
- Number of defective plastic caps per day

- Number of car drivers not wearing seat belts at a given point per day

Data on relative merit or points is more subjective but can be used to rank perceptions. Checksheets are simply tables drawn up in columns and rows with headlines related to the process. All that is required is a simple tick or dash in a box to accurately record events. The design of these must be:

- Simple
- Clear
- Effective
- Easily read and filled in

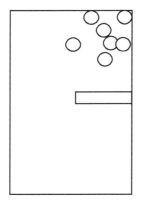

Date		Operator
Type		
Model		Paint
Size		

1 dot = 1 defect

Figure 6.5 Production checksheet.

6.8 Run Charts

Run charts are graphs of a variable against time. For example, if we wish to know how the temperature of a furnace is varying with time, we can plot a run chart or temperature and record it each hour. An example is given in Figure 6.6.

This figure has particular significance. The production of cars in the USA has a sinusoidal appearance. The production in Japan shows a continuous increase. The US strategy and tactics clearly did not work. The US designed cars for the USA not the world, the Japanese designed cards for the world.

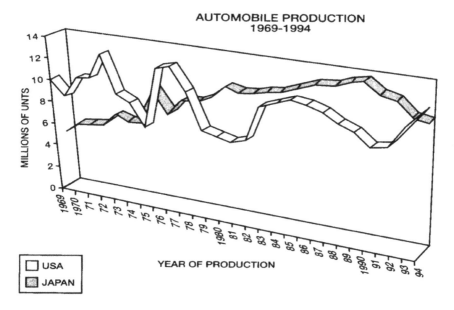

Figure 6.6 Auto production 1969 to 1994.

6.9 Frequency Distribution (Histogram) and the Normal Distribution

A histogram is a plot of the frequency of an occurrence against a measurement. A histogram is another very useful tool to produce a mind picture to aid understanding. It leads to a probability density function and ultimately the normal distribution if special causes of variation are removed or the sample size consists of only common causes. This bell-shaped curve is illustrated in Figure 6.7. Figure 6.8 is the same data presented as a run chart.

An added help for data that in its raw form is not normal is that if averages are taken then the distribution will be normal as shown in Figure 6.9.

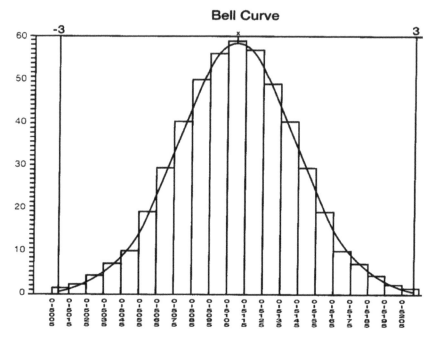

Figure 6.7 Normal distribution.

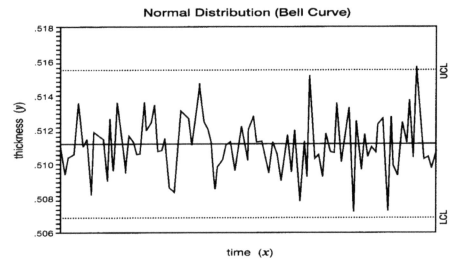

Figure 6.8 Run chart for the Bell Curve data in Figure 6.7.

Averages of All Distribution are Normal

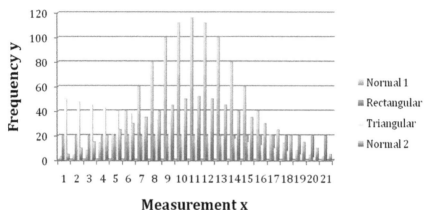

Figure 6.9 Bell Curve for averages of non-normal distributions.

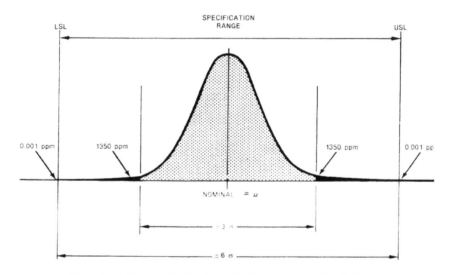

Figure 6.10 Normal distribution with 0.001 ppm outside Six Sigma.

6.10   Magic Lanterns

Moroney, in "Facts from Figures", says that cold figures are uninspiring to most people. Diagrams, however, help us to see the pattern and shape of a complex situation.

Give me an undigested heap of figures and it is difficult to see the wood for the trees. Give me a diagram and I am encouraged to forget the detail until I have a real gasp of the big picture.

An example of a magic lantern is given in Figure 6.11. The message is clear; we are heading for disaster.

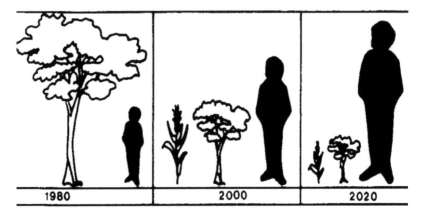

| 1980 | 2000 | 2020 |

Figure 6.11 Example of a magic lantern. The figure is taken from "How to Save The World", a Strategy for World Conservation by Robert Allen.

6.11 Statistics

By statistics, we mean simply measurement data. Historically, statistics is state arithmetic (data calculated by the state-census). It is a system of computations based on averages. It is about variability and probability. It is about inferring characteristics of a population from measurements of a sample. There are a few points to note:

- We can never find the true value
- No two measurements (of the same or of different things) will ever be exactly the same
- We live in a world of dispersion
- To describe a collection of data, we need a measure of the:
    - Central forming tendency (the average = xbar)
    - Range (R) (maximum value minus minimum value)
- There will always be a dispersion or spread

If the curve is not a symmetrical bell-shaped one (normal distribution) and is a combination of, say, a rectangular or triangle distribution and a bell curve, then the result is a distorted bell distribution then we need a measurement of:

- Mean (average)
- Mode (most likely score)
- Median (middle score)

6.12 Stratification

The process of taking general data and splitting it up into its component parts is called stratification. Examples:

- A defect rate for 500 plastic mouldings is 30 (6%). If we split this into each moulding machine, then the problem is more readily solved. Further stratification into operators or shift times will also help.

- Likewise, when two different raw materials are used, say, in the same process then it is clear that they should be treated separately, but often as a starting point all the data is aggregated so the first step is to stratify the data.

6.13 Scatter Diagrams

The scatter diagram is useful in visually showing the correlation that exists between two measurements: x the independent variable and y the dependent variable. By convention, y is plotted vertically and x is plotted horizontally.

For example, in the medical profession, we might want to know the relationship between smoking cigarettes (number per day) and cancer deaths per 100,000 people or, between coffee consumption and heart attack deaths per 100,000 people. For smoking, the graph would look like Figure 6.12. The trend line indicates that the more tobacco we consume the greater the probability of our life being shortened. We do not need to be a medical practitioner to interpret this graph. Again this illustrates the power of a simple graphical approach – magic?

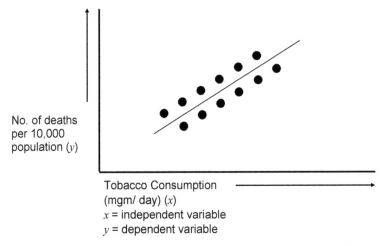

No. of deaths
per 10,000
population (y)

Tobacco Consumption
(mgm/ day) (x)
x = independent variable
y = dependent variable

Figure 6.12 Relationship between death rate and tobacco consumption.

6.14   Cause and Effect Diagrams

The basic cause and effect diagram, or Ishikawa diagram, is illustrated in Figure 6.13. Once again, it is a magic lantern to aid team problem-solving. The diagram is used as follows:

Step 1: State the problem (define as precisely as possible)

Step 2: Decide on grouping (men, materials, machines, method)

  • Special (specific to problems)

Step 3: Brainstorm for causes

  • One per turn
  • Five whys and how (who, why, what, where, when and how)
  • Creativity stimulates causes
  • Causes are added as a branch to the diagram
  • All pass- brainstorming over

Step 4: Critically examine causes

  • Identify best causes
  • Look for deviations/changes

Step 5: Rank most probable causes in order of importance

  • Top cause in No. 1
  • Verification test (brainstorm)

Step 6: (Optional)

- Prepare a large board (magic lantern) and display new machine or process. Hang the 'standard method' on each arm of the diagram. Place it near the machine (the source of the data).

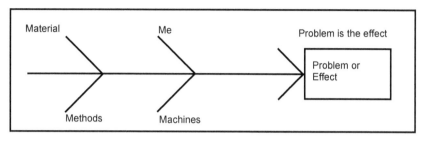

Australians like to call this "DEAD NED" after bushranger Ned Kelly who wore a large rectangular steel helmet when he was ambushed by police last century.

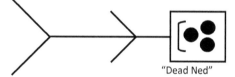

Figure 6.13 Cause and effect diagram.

Cause and Effect Diagrams

- It is important to understand a problem clearly, knowing all the causes of the problem before making a counter-plan – the cause and effect diagram will help understanding.
- It is important to know the systematic causes and related sub-causes which affect the manufacturing process.
- The cause and effect diagram can give hints for possible improvements.
- The cause and effect diagram is a checklist for studying the cause and effect relationships.

6.15   Pareto Charts

In the 19th Century, Vilfredo Pareto devised this method to organise data so that the most influential causes of a problem could be easily recognised. This approach used a bar graph to put in rank order the various factors that contribute to the total problem. The Pareto chart 'identifies the 'significant few' from the 'trivial many'.

How to Make a Pareto Chart

1. Divide the problem into various factors
2. Make a data table of these factors: rank factors from top to bottom in order with the frequently occurring factors first
3. Calculate the percent and cumulative percentage for each factor
4. Make a bar graph for all factors using the percent column, and add a line graph for all factors using the cumulative column
5. As a general rule, divide the cumulative curve into three segments (A, B and C) at the points on the curve which corresponds to 70% and 95%. Factors included within segment. A will be the target for improvement.

Special Points About Pareto charts

1. If a number of causes contribute to a single effect, it is always the case that there will be a small proportion of the causes that contribute to the majority of the effect
2. 80/20 rule – 20% of the causes is responsible for 80% of the effect
3. We can divide the Pareto chart into 3 regions A, B and C for error analysis

Table 6.1 Tabulated data in order of priority for the reasons why cars breakdown (from many sources)

Your car's most common problems		
Problem	Number	Percentage
1. Battery	7.833	35.3
2. Electrical	3.276	14.8
3. Fuel	2.769	12.5
4. Ignition	2.491	11.2
5. Locked out	2.194	9.9
6. Cooling	972	4.4
7. Wheel change	741	3.3
8. Engine	535	2.4
9. Other	1.374	6.2
Total	**22,185**	

*Notice that problems 1, 3 and 5 (over 50%) could probably be most avoided if the vehicle was maintained with greater care.

If a number of causes contribute to a single effect, it is always the case that there will be a small proportion of causes that contribute to the majority of the effect.

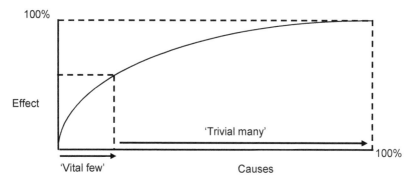

Figure 6.14 Cumulative Pareto chart.

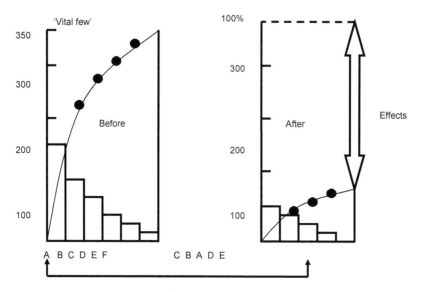

Figure 6.15 A Pareto chart (bar chart and cumulative graph).

6.16 Team Problem-Solving

There are numerous team problem-solving exercises around that illustrate that the team is most often better at providing answers than even the best individual. Of the many exercises I have supervised, not once has a team failed to out-perform the average individual score of a group. Occasionally individuals will outperform the team, but the fact remains that the team will out-perform the average individual score of the groups. The success of this depends a lot on psychology and technique, but it can all be learned. Part of the team problem-solving technique is to teach teams to extract the best information from the people so that all might benefit and the group synergises.

6.17   Control Charts

Once the correct measurements are put in place and all the obvious causes of variation are removed, the next management tool to use is the control chart, discussed in great detail by Dr. Shewhart and Dr. Deming. This chart is a run chart with both variation limits and specification limits drawn on them. It is important for all people involved to understand the difference between these two ideas. The process sets the variation limits while the customer or the next process sets the specification limits.

The target dimension plus or minus three standard deviations (Sigma) sets the upper and lower variation limits which are called the control limits. A standard deviation is defined as the square root of the sum of the differences between the reading and the average divided by the number of measurement minus one. For the system to be under statistical control, the process variation must be inside the limits at least 99.7%. Such charts will lead to 0.3% defective products or outputs. This system is no longer good enough in complex systems where processes in series can greatly amplify errors.

The statistical capability of the process with plus or minus. Three Sigma, if the measurements are within the control limits 99.7% of the time is mathematically one. Here the capability is defined as the difference in the specification limits divided by six standard deviations. In manufacturing processes to operate at plus or minus Six Sigma the defect rate outside these limits would be 0.001 ppm, or one part per billion. Practically this is almost impossible to achieve in most plants so that Motorola devised what they called Six Sigma processes which allow for a 1.5 Sigma shift in the target and then a defect rate of 3 ppm.

A typical simple control chart is shown in Figure 6.16. Here, the average and the range in the measurement in the sample are plotted. This process is rapidly going out of control so action is required.

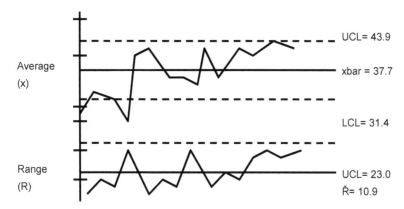

Figure 6.16 Control chart with variation limits at Three Sigma. This is an xbar (average): R (Range) chart for a variable x versus time the UCL (Upper Control Limits) and LCL (Lower Control Limits) have been plotted.

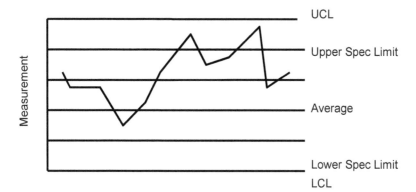

Figure 6.17 R Chart with specification limits.

The UCL and LCL represent the variations expected for the process without special causes present. 99.7% of all measurement should be within these UCL and LCL limits. For the above control chart, the upper and lower specification limits are inside the UCL and LCL. This is unsatisfactory. It means the process variation is too large.

6.18 Reducing Variation to Three Sigma and Then Six Sigma

The procedure to establish an average and range chart is as follows:

1. Randomly select items for measurement
2. Calculate Range (R) and Average (xbar)

Analyse the histogram and chart and brainstorm to find special causes (causes of variation that can be identified). These are any non-random factors causing variation inconsistent with the variation to be expected from the pure chance of common causes; that is the variation to be expected if the process was in statistical control.

Unless all the special causes of variation are identified and corrected, they will continue to affect the process output in unpredictable ways. They cannot, therefore, be planned for and must be identified and eliminated first. When the special assignable causes have been eliminated, the remaining variation is the natural variation of the process. This represents the natural variation in process output which is to be expected, and can therefore be planned for.

When the process is under statistical control (between UCL and LCL 99.7% of the time), we need to look at ways of further reducing variation to head for Six Sigma. This involves investigating the design of the process and in manufacturing carrying out experiments designed to assist in prioritising the design elements that are likely to cause the variation. Experimental design is available to assist.

Kaizen means improve, improve, improve. Dr. Shewhart, and later Dr. Deming, used the Standardise Do Check Act (SDCA) wheel to illustrate this. Aim for constant and never-ending improvement as we continue to turn this wheel to aim for precision to achieve cycle-time reduction and higher-velocity. Three Sigma for manufacturing processes (plus or minus Three Sigma) is not good enough with today's technology. Aim for the Six Sigma specified as plus or minus Six Sigma with a target shift of 1.5 Sigma; that is, a defect rate of 3.0 parts per million.

This is particularly so for upstream manufacturing processes. Ultimately if the customer specification limits are broad, a greater amount of variation is tolerable, but there are still substantial benefits in reducing variation since when the variation is reduced more opportunities for further innovation present themselves, as shown in Figure 6.18. Each jump in productivity occurs when the previous process variation is reduced after the elimination of special assignable causes of variation.

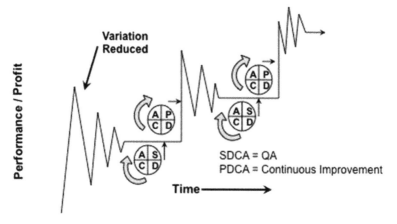

Figure 6.18 Performance improvement.

As the Shewhart-Deming wheel rotates to continuously reduce variation, further inspiration and creativity results in a leap in productivity and profitability. This continuous improvement when fed into the supply chain will result in a significant reduction in cycle-time and an increase in velocity of the movement of goods and services to the customer. To achieve this, all processes must operate at a high degree of precision, and people must work on harmony to synergise creativity. It is about people, process and precision to achieve maximum velocity.

The Internet has changed our life in every way. Artificial Intelligence, (AI), is all around us and now guiding us almost unnoticed. It has been readily accepted as it fused with our way of life. In particular, it has been the precursor to what has been defined as Smart Manufacturing, which in itself uses all the elements of our rich imagination. Most of us are familiar with

Alexa or Siri. Climate change, the resultant use of renewables, rapid globalisation are all being fuelled by the tools of what is loosely called the Fourth Industrial Revolution or what is called Industry 4.0.

The Internet of Things (IoT), wide use of sensors, robotics and machine to machine communication, can lead to the complete replacement of old methods of batch manufacturing with something approaching continuous flow. Smart machines can analyse and diagnose issues without the need for human intervention or at least continuously monitor situations to predict and help prevent catastrophic failure. Virtual Reality (VR) can supply diagnostic and fault fixing methodologies through the glasses to the user for instant understanding and remedy of problems. The Japanese ideal of total prevention of failure can possibly be achieved. However, the fundamental framework the business must be in place.

Chapter 7

The Future of Business and Manufacturing

Summary

Artificial Intelligence, big data, the Internet of Things, cloud computing, robots, Statistical Process Control (SPC), virtual reality machine learning, and sensorisation will continue to have an accelerated impact on every part of our daily lives. For business and manufacturing it is the fast future. The new generation of computers using quantum technology will accelerate the change process even more.

7.1 Accelerated Change

The overarching world activity is accelerating change in 4 areas: technology, economy, society, and the planet. The technology changes have been expressed as Industry 4.0. Included here are: increased use of the cloud, additive manufacturing, autonomous robots, simulation models, horizontal and vertical integration, cybersecurity, the Internet of everything, big data and machine learning, and artificial intelligence (AI). Economy includes slower growth, USA vs. China, Brexit and increasing protectionism. Society has the future of work, less jobs, gig economy and inequality.

Technology for Business: Application of the Advances in Industry 4.0 to Small to Medium Sized Enterprises
John Blakemore
Copyright © 2023 Jenny Stanford Publishing Pte. Ltd.
ISBN 978-981-4968-70-6 (Hardcover), 978-1-003-38216-4 (eBook)
www.jennystanford.com

The planet includes global warming, polluted oceans, pandemics and countries having water shortages.

Today's products, such as industrial machines, cars, planes and complex medical equipment, have become ultra-sophisticated cyber-physical systems. 10 years ago, cars had around 10 to 15 electronic control units (ECUs). Today that number is > 90. In some luxury cars, it's as high as 150. Mercedes in the mid-90s had 8 models. Now they have >20, and on each of these, build and trim options far exceed past models. Today's products are changing more rapidly than ever before and doing so to cater for the increasing expectations of customers. This is happening to all industries. Today's customers expect connected products with sophisticated software-driven features. The products are expected to be delivered at a lower cost, with better performance and developed in much shorter timescales than ever before.

To meet the above requirements, manufacturing companies, world-wide, have had to adjust their operations to meet the increasing complex requirements. Both the World Economic Forum (WEF) and McKinsey Consultants in an ongoing research project have created the Global Lighthouse Network, in order, to meet the above requirements. In 2018, the WEF identified 16 companies as Fourth Industrial Revolution (4IR) leaders for their work in scaling digital use cases beyond the pilot phase across individual sites: these sites were designated as advanced manufacturing "Lighthouses".

In 2019, a further 28 facilities were identified and added to the network, bringing the total to 44. Even more significantly, some companies are generating value from 4IR technologies far beyond the 4 walls of their factories: 14 of these 28 new sites have been recognised as end-to-end (E2E) lighthouses, integrating manufacturing innovation from their suppliers through to their customers.

The 44 designated factories show remarkable diversity. They arise across industries, sectors and geographies, ranging from single-site SMEs to some of the world's largest corporations. See Table 7.1 for an example of performances.

The use of sophisticated CAD systems is becoming mandatory for complex products. Systems driven product development have proven to be valuable methodologies. These are supported by

Product Lifecycle Management (PLM) systems which address product complexity and variability, optimisation and traceability. These systems lower the barriers between disciplines and integrating environments across electrical, electronic and mechanical disciplines. For an example of a sophisticated CAD system.

Table 7.1 Impact of the use of the tools of the Fourth Industrial Revolution

	KPI improvement	Impact observed
Productivity	Increase in factory output	10 to 200%
	Productivity increase	5 to 160%
	Operational effectiveness	3 to 50%
	Quality cost reduction	5 to 90%
	Product cost reduction	5 to 40%
Agility	Energy efficiency	2 to 50%
	Inventory reduction	10 to 90%
	Lead time reduction	10 to 90%
	Time to market reduction	30 to 90%
	Change over reduction	30 to 70%
Customisation	Lot size reduction	50 to 90%

The above changes to manufacturing are presenting a real challenge to Australian manufacturing, especially to the SMEs, who play a very important role in Australia's economy, more so than in other developed nations.

7.2 Current Situation Using Australia as an Example

Australia is a country of small businesses. The manufacturing industry is no exception. It has gone through a long decline when it was about 30% of the country's GDP in 1960 down to < 6%. In recent years, it has lost the automotive industry with its design teams, automation and strong management. Manufacturing can be a great source of jobs for both professionals, tradesmen and unskilled people, as well as a potential exporter and a source of intellectual property (IP) through Research and Development (R&D). The Small to Medium Sized Enterprises (SME's) perform poorly when it comes to exporting as Australian SMEs export 14% of their output against the G7 countries who export about 25% and the European companies export about 35% but the Australia's manufacturing SMEs export performance is poor as only 4.5% of the companies export which is 4% of the value of the manufacturing industry.

The writers used to collect the many Government reports on both manufacturing and innovation. In fact, there have been about 60 reports on each subject produced since the war. But both manufacturing and innovation have declined?

The most recent article commented that since 2002, the most productive Australian firms (top 5%) had not kept pace with the most productive firms globally. Australia's productivity has slipped back by about 33%. For the past 2 decades, the other 95% of firms "output per hour" has barely risen. The article raised: What's going wrong? Part of the problem is that many firms aren't investing in new technologies. The Productivity Commission's report: it's not just that companies aren't investing simply in technology – *they're not investing in anything at all!* Also, across the economy, businesses are cutting back on R&D and investing less in good management. Just 8% of firms say they produce innovations that are new, down from 11% in 2013. The Commission has found that 50% of the slowdown in productivity improvement in the market economy in recent years is accounted for by manufacturing!

Newborn firms are as critical to an economy who bring fresh approaches, shaking up existing industries and offering new opportunities to workers. Defining new businesses as those that employ one worker. Treasury estimates that the new business formation rate in the early 2000s was 14% a year. Now it's down to 11% a year. The CSIRO Futures report comments that, industry and research should focus on addressing: Risk averse culture, segregated national agenda, poor commercialisation and quality and quantity of leaders. On top of this is, manufacturing industry has a high cost labour-force and high electrical supply/energy costs.

An interesting report by the AMGC (The Advanced Manufacturing Growth Centre), based in South Australia, found that Australia is home to one of the most volatile manufacturing industries in the world. AMGC found that 40% of Australian Manufacturers do not even have a website.

Collaboration between universities and Australian manufacturers is poor with only about 4% of manufacturers have R&D collaborations with universities.

The writers experience of Australian manufacturing companies is that large companies do not need Government help as they can afford consultants to help them with strategy, innovation and operations. They can also obtain investment from banks/investors and have professional management. Also, many of them are overseas-owned and are monopolies or oligopolies.

The future of Australian manufacturing is the medium-sized companies, where there are about 6,500 of them, and, who are generally Australian-owned, have reasonably good management and they export. The challenge for them is to adopt Industry 4.0 and its elements as quickly as possible. They can get funding from the banking sectors and use Government help with new product development, process innovation and the use of the knowledge and experience from the consultants. However, this crucial segment has suffered a catastrophic decline in the last 12 years of about 36%!

With regards, to the small manufacturing companies, this is manufacturing's *weak link* as they have untrained management, limited finances, generally, cannot afford new product development and are not market-oriented and do-little market research. Many do not have professional engineers. Also, they cannot afford consultants! Many are dependent on one or two major customers! They also do not like to get Government help.

Many Government schemes involve a dollar from the company matched to a dollar from the Government. A well-publicised scheme for R&D and product creation. This is called the "Accelerating Commercial" Grant which can go up to $1 million for eligible companies. This is more suitable for large and medium sized companies. The writer has found that many manufacturers, especially, the small companies do not have the matching dollars.

Overall, much has been done to help manufacturing industry, but it has continued to decline. However, there is a promising industry sector, the medical technologies, the pharmaceutical industry and the biotech sector. This sector is supported by a world-class medical research capability.

7.3   Improving Manufacturing

To improve Australia's manufacturing industry for the country's economic future is a large and complex task.

Little has happened after all the above reports. The writers believe that the Federal Government will not spend a lot of money. This means that we must use the organisations in existence to transform Australian manufacturing!

The writers believe the answer to improving Australia's manufacturing industry should be based on four sequential strategies: (1) Educating SMEs management; (2) the creation of new products and processes; (3) Improving the productivity and performance and (4) Creation of new Manufacturing Companies.

1. Educating Management:

    Let us look at the major part of manufacturing, the "small company" sector. The writers believe from experience working with small companies, the major issue is the ignorance of management of the owners/CEOs. As they cannot afford management consultants, they must look for a cheaper way of getting the management knowledge. This can come from two sources, (1) The TAFES and (2) "The Small Business Mentoring Service" based in Melbourne. This organisation has about 150 mentors, male and female, who are ex-CEOs and business owners who are volunteers and get a small fee for each session they deliver. The cost to a company for four mentor sessions is a modest $320. This organisation operates in three states, Victoria, NSW and Tasmania. Using the TAFEs mean attending classes, this is difficult to get time off when you are very busy running your operation! The latter approach is the way to go where they can get cheap mentoring help from experienced mentors during working hours.

The SMEs need an infusion of fresh talent, for innovation and management, this could come from more engineers and MBAs. Currently, there are about 50,000 engineers working in the manufacturing industry. The Engineers Australia (EA) claim about 38,711 engineers working in the industry (10) but not all engineers are registered with the EA. There are about 47,530 employing manufacturing companies in Australia. This means that there are about 1.05 engineers per manufacturing company. Not many small companies employ engineers as most of them work in the medium and large companies. Returning to the MBAs, again very few MBAs work in the manufacturing industry. The reason is that the financial rewards are in the financial services. The writers doubt that there are few MBAs in the small manufacturing sector because the MBAs salary expectations are high, at say about $100,000 per year. One of the problems with the manufacturing sector is that many SME companies are managed by tradesmen with little management training! Bringing in more engineers and MBAs would cause a culture problem for existing SME CEOs and owners. Unfortunately, many of the owners are aging as 60% of them are over 47 to middle 60s and upwards.

2. The creation of new Products:

Another issue for Small to Medium sized Enterprises is that an Ai (Australian Industry) Group article found that in 2019, the most popular strategy was "introducing new products/services" with 30% of CEOs ranking this as their first response. Creating new products/services is a complex task. In 2018, a study from CSIRO, found that a "new to market" when a company invests in their own novel products, only 5.5% of Australian businesses were doing this! Even large businesses find this to be very difficult as a McKinsey study found that 94% of executives around the world are dissatisfied with their firms' innovation performance. A newsletter from the AGMC said that Australia is falling behind in the global innovation race. The newsletter also commented that an ISA report found that just one in three Australian businesses spends money on innovation (encompassing R&D, digitalisation, staff training etc.) and just 6% of Australian businesses invest in pure R&D.

Another problem for companies trying to create new products is that world-wide they have a poor success rate. Only about 20% survive longer than a year and new product launches are 6 times more expensive than line extension launches. The result: as many as 95% of new products introduced each year fail. A recent study by Lifecycle Insights on product development success confirms that companies are struggling with sub-optimal product development practices as a scant 13% of all design projects launch on time without significant changes to resource allocation. The reality is that 45% of all design projects are either cancelled or miss their product launch date to any number of reasons – among them, failed prototypes, incorrectly ordered parts or manufacturing issues.

This strategy is by far the most difficult strategy of the three to implement. A possible approach is to copy the UK where the Design Council provided a high-level design coaching to > 2,300 SMEs through a program called "Designing Demand". The purpose of this BIS-funded program has been to counteract a lack of design capability. A study in 2011 showed that every AU$1 invested in a design project returned > AU$25 within a 2-year period. Benefits have been accelerated growth and increased market share.

Australia should copy the UK in having a similar program. The "Good Design Australia" organisation should set up a program for Australia like the "Designing Demand" program using the Swinburne University of Technology's "Advanced Manufacturing & Design Centre" in cooperation with the AMGC to run a design coaching program for SMEs. Fortunately, the Victorian Government set up the "Design2Thrive" program in 2018. Its objective is to drive profitable and sustainable growth for Victorian companies.

The program is an interactive 12-month immersion in design-led thinking across strategy, culture, marketing and product design. After the program, the SMEs can get design help from the high-quality Design agencies; e.g., Cobaltniche, Ingenuity, Boost Design, Bayly Design Group and Cobalt Design, in the capital cities.

Hopefully, the new products created by the SMEs would give them a fillip in the world's markets.

A major issue for creating new products is the cost of doing so which can cost about $2 million and take about 2 years. The Federal Government must help the small companies with loans which can be paid back over a 10-year period. This is a very difficult task (see Table 7.2).

Table 7.2 Product design and manufacture

User requirements	Design and manufacture	Post production
1. User needs satisfied	10. In house or outsource	19. Warranty policy
2. Target users	11. Concept and drawings	20. Tech support
3. Product features	12. Simulation	21. Selling price
4.Performance required	13. Tooling	22. Manufacturing cost
5. Design brief	14. Prototype	23. Distribution
6. Environment	15. Flexibility in design	24. Development budget
7. Reliability, quality	16. Documentation	25. Capital expenditure
8. Patent issues	17. Manufacture	26. Product launch
9. Safety, compliance	18. Launch date	27. Lead time

7.4 Improving the Productivity

The major approach to improving manufacturing operations is called "Lean" which was developed from JIT from Japan and Industrial Engineering in the USA. Another two approaches are Six Sigma and TQM. These traditional levers have driven productivity in the last 60 years but are starting to run out of steam and the incremental benefits they deliver are declining. (20)

Fortunately, the AMGC has initiated a project which has pulled in the Department of Industry's Entrepreneur Program and involved SME's together to deliver an initiative with great potential for its participants. It is using Dematec Automation, a South Australian company, which is an automation and Industry 4.0 specialist based in Adelaide. 17 Australian SME manufacturers are being helped to integrate Internet of Things (IoT) capability into their products or retrofit legacy machinery with Industry 4.0-style instrumentation. This provides participants with a way to inexpensively lift their IT intensity and to understand internal and external applications of digital adoption. They have developed an IoT platform that enables us to deliver digitalisation services to clients across all sectors at a very cost-effective price point. Dematec believes that adopting Industry 4.0 technologies combining solutions such as sensors, cloud computing and analytics, is essential for manufacturing's competitiveness. AMGC has contributed about $250,000 and industry the same amount. Another benefit of Industry 4.0 technologies could be the potential of "right-shoring" where some of a company's components which were made offshore could now be made in Australia! This is a great project to increase competitiveness in SMEs. This very important initiative shows that the combination of Government resources and industries involvement is a guide to the future success of manufacturing industry.

A recent report on "Industry 4.0 Success" stated that *50% of IoT projects are failing*. According to research, the missing step is often setting an "enterprise strategy" for the transformation. Industry 4.0 is far broader than the manufacturing plant's operations and processes. Every department + the ecosystem of suppliers, distributors and partners are involved. Only with an enterprise-level transformation can manufacturers design, prioritise and execute projects with assurance that they will build toward Industry 4.0. The report outlines Essential Steps toward Success:

1. Develop a vision with significant benefits for all stakeholders.
2. Craft a strategy with Industry 4.0 as part of the way to achieve those benefits. Explain the enterprise's purpose, priorities, metrics, targets, principles and standards.

3. Create specific stories for each group of stakeholders to see their benefits.
4. Set standards. Designate standard owners such as managers to encourage, support and enable use.
5. Foster a new mindset. Help people shift from fear into curiosity with shifts in incentives, structures, metrics and examples from leaders anywhere in the organisation.

The Federal Government have introduced an "Advanced Manufacturing Fund" worth $100 million which meets the above objectives of creating more digitised manufacturing but considering the amount of SMEs and their need for consulting help in the complex implementation, the $100 million will need to be increased to about $500 million.

7.5   Creation of New Manufacturing Companies

Starting a new company is also very difficult, when it is a manufacturing company, as the founder will need to create a suitable product followed by a line of other suitable products. This is not an easy task! Just starting a jobbing shop is not the same.

There are 3 stages for a start-up:

1. Problem-solving idea
2. Development of the idea
3. Growth, of the business idea.

Ideas can come from anywhere, e.g., working in an industry and seeing a need which is not being met, new technologies and university spin-offs.

The press promotes the start-ups of young people but the ideal age according to a recent study of 2.7 million founders in the USA by the USA Census Bureau and MIT Professors found that the most successful entrepreneurs tend to be middle-aged (average age was 45), even in the tech sector. (23) The writer who has been involved with > 100 start-ups confirms the above data about entrepreneurs. Also, many young people have little experience of growing a company. Experience has shown that the failure rate of start-ups can be about 90%. However, private Accelerators are available to help advance existing start-ups where the founders get help with their start-up for about 3 months + obtain some investment. Their success rate is better than the 10% above. Currently, a recent initiative in NSW is very promising where an entrepreneur has created an Accelerator for manufacturing called "The Melt" which offers 4 features:

1. Process for the product development
2. Tools and service and access to a mechatronic engineering laboratory worth $3 million, design studios
3. Coworking and expertise where there is a team of about 20 engineers
4. International linkages. On top of these features, is that each start-up team get an investment of $150,00 plus caters for existing manufacturing companies looking to create new products. there are 5 start-ups in operation. There has been much research world-wide on success factors for start-ups but about 5 years ago surprising research showed that the most crucial success factor is "timing" of the start-ups (see Table 7.3).

Table 7.3 Top 5 success factors for manufacturing businesses

1	Timing	42%
2	Team/Execution	32%
3	Ideas	28%
4	Business Model	24%
5	Funding	

Creating a new manufacturing company is possibly more complex than a company creating new products.

A recent report by Deloitte's Access Economics for LaunchVic called "Productivity is not an accident" covered the subject of "The economics and impact of Victoria's start-up ecosystem". The report estimates the revenue of the Victorian start-up industry to be in the order of $4.6 billion in 2019 based on 1,670 start-ups and scale-ups. The ABS and Deloitte estimates, the value-added of the start-up industry is $2.4 billion. The industry contributes around 0.6% to the Victorian economy. The report's findings indicate that the % of start-ups in manufacturing is a poor 1.2% which has high specialisation ratio of 1.2 which is a measure of Victoria's competitive advantage!

7.6   Conclusions

A large part of the decline of manufacturing industry in Australia can be attributed to politicians and management as they did not adopt much of the many reports on innovation and manufacturing in the last 60 years. A lot of the decline occurred in the crucial medium-sized manufacturing companies.

However, there are some bright spots, the medical technologies, pharmaceutical and biotech sector, a few companies like ANCA and CSL where both could qualify to be a "Lighthouse" company and during the Coronavirus pandemic, a few Australian manufacturing companies have risen to the challenge of manufacturing medical protective equipment. The medical technologies, pharmaceutical and biotech sector is supported by world-class medical research institutes.

Interestingly, President Obama announced an investment of a US$1 billion in a National Network for Manufacturing Innovation (NNMI). The key focus is on new technology paradigms that can improve the competitiveness of American manufacturing – with a focus on SMEs – through digitisation of design and manufacturing, democratising of technology and collaborative design and analytics to sustain leadership across US manufacturing ecosystem. This approach is similar to Germany's Fraunhofer Institutes.

A very recent Industrial Manufacturing trends report by PWC made the important point that for these companies to succeed through the current pandemic where their demands will be reduced and CEOs must resize their companies to accommodate this, they also will have to focus on creating agility so that they can pivot to meet changing conditions and they must strengthen their technological capabilities across functions by reorganising their supply chains and building a workforce with Industry 4.0 skill sets!

Manufacturing is an industry of the future where it uses its citizens education, training and experience, creates well-paid jobs (about 1 million of them) and is a great source of exports and IP.

One of the conclusions from this paper is that creating new products by manufacturing companies and the creation of new manufacturing companies is a complex business with a low success factor. A recent report on start-ups in Victoria found that % of start-ups in manufacturing was a low 1.2% where Victoria is a major manufacturing state. This reveals that university engineering departments and engineers/managers are letting down the manufacturing industry!

For the future, to promote the manufacturing industry the government must create Australia-wide design programs and be prepared to support small and medium sized manufacturing companies when they try to create new products with significant amounts of money, possibly in the hundreds of millions of dollars.

The idea of the three strategies (1 to 3) is to grow some of the better small manufacturing companies into medium-sized companies as well as grow the better medium-sized companies into large companies. With regards to start-ups, again, the Government should create a body to coordinate start-ups throughout Australia. Also, the Federal Government, needs to increase the Advanced Manufacturing Fund to about $500 million.

The above strategies will take time to implement but a quicker approach would be a commitment from state and federal Governments to increased levels of local content for all procurement decisions; e.g. rail industry projects. As recently as 10 years ago most rail vehicles were designed and manufactured here in Australia but not anymore.

It would appear, that the combination of a lack of Government help in applying strategies to help manufacturing, untrained management and the difficulty of creating new products and new companies + high exchange rates, rise of China's manufacturing industry, high wage costs, lack of skilled workers and high energy costs, is the reason for the decline of the industry in the last 60 years. The growth of the manufacturing industry in the future is restrained by the above difficulties.

The aim of this chapter is to create a stronger manufacturing industry in Australia, in order, to strengthen Australia's economic future and to create jobs.

References

1. The new logic of competition, R. Kimura, M. Reeves & K. Whitaker, BCG, 15 February 2020.

2. Deliver quality, fast & informed designs, Siemens Digital Industries Software, 5 February 2020.

3. Industry's fast-mover advantage: Enterprise value from digital factories, F. Betti, E. de Boer & Y. Giraud, McKinsey & Company, January 2020.

4. Australian Small Business & Family Enterprise Ombudsman, Small Business Counts 2019, page 41.

5. Productivity issue? Let's start @ the bottom, not the top, R. Gittins, Business, Age, 2 March 2020, page 23.

6. CSIRO Futures, Manufacturing, May 2019.

7. AMGC, Building Resilience in Australian Manufacturing, J. Goennemann, 2018.

8. Collaborating to gain a competitive advantage, events, MM, February 2019.

9. The Engineering Profession, A Statistical Overview, 14th Edition, Engineers Australia, June 2019.

10. Victoria leading the way, W. Noonan, Manufacturing Monthly, July 2017, page 7.

11. Australian Manufacturing in 2019, AiGroup, May 2019, page 16.

12. The perfect age to become CEO, L. Main, Financial Review, 15 September 2020.

13. Australian Manufacturing in 2019, AiGroup, May 2019, page 5.

14. The last word, To develop, create & grow, L. Marshall, CSIRO, Manufacturing Monthly, March 2018, page 42.

15. Breaking the barriers to Innovation, S. D. Anthony, P. Cobban, HBR, November-December 2019.

16. Newsletter, A message from Jens Goennemann, AMGC, 5/3/2020.

17. How to successfully bring New Products to Market, L. Patterson, VisionEdge Marketing, Industryweek.com, 1 September 2018.

18. Cloud-Enabled Digital Transformation of Product Development, Lifecycle Insights, Dassault Systemes, Solidworks, 4 May 2020.

19. A Business Innovation Infrastructure with Design Inside, Design for Innovation, Design Council, December 2011, page 10.

20. Adopting disruptive digital technologies in making & delivering, K. Goering, R. Kelly & N. Mellors, McKinsey & Company, 2018.

21. Industry 4.0 digitisation of SME infrastructure, www.dematec.com. au/june-11-2019.html, 23/03/2020.

22. Why Strategy Matters to Industry 4.0 Success, J. Fraser, Tech-Clarity, June 2020.

23. A study of 2.7m start-ups found the ideal age to start a business (& its much older than you think), J. Haden, June 2019.

24. A new accelerator, The Melt, is cranking up Australian manufacturing after investing in 5 start-ups, www.startupdaily.net, 21 September 2020.

25. Productivity is not an accident, The economics & impact of Victoria's start-up ecosystem, Deloitte Access Economics, June 2020.

26. Developing the Digital Manufacturing Commons: A National Initiative for US Manufacturing Innovation, B. Beckman, A. Giani, J. Carbone, P. Koudal, J. Salvo and J. Barkley, Elsevier, Procedia Manufacturing, Volume 5, 2016.

27. Industrial manufacturing trends 2020: Succeeding in uncertainty through agility & innovation, 23rd Annual Global CEO Survey: trend report, PwC, June 2020.

Chapter 8

Project Results

Summary

This chapter details some of the projects where business and manufacturing processes have been improved using many of the tools described earlier. In all cases the permission of the client was sought and given. There is no limit to the type of manufacturing process to which the rules of industry 4.0 can be applied. The processes range from plastic injection moulding to cement manufacture to medical devices.

8.1   Results from Project at Precision

(*Dr. Bob Blake gave permission to use this data.*)

The 12-Step Implementation Plan described earlier was implemented. At the start of the project, the company was planning to buy a further 14 injection moulding machines. At the end of the project, productivity of the existing machines and the quality of the output had improved to such an extent that this capital expenditure was not necessary. The results are displayed in Figure 8.1.

- This graph shows unusual but significant characteristics. All measurements were done using sampling in accordance with military and international standards. The measurements up to Week 5 were historical.

Technology for Business: Application of the Advances in Industry 4.0 to Small to Medium Sized Enterprises
John Blakemore
Copyright © 2023 Jenny Stanford Publishing Pte. Ltd.
ISBN 978-981-4968-70-6 (Hardcover), 978-1-003-38216-4 (eBook)
www.jennystanford.com

- At Week 5, the process was examined in detail and it was found that the measurement system was in error. Every time the injection moulding machine went through a cycle and a defect appeared then the cavity in the mould where it occurred was blocked off.

- This process was continued till approximately 50% of all the cavities were not producing nylon valves but the machine was still doing work as if it was producing twice as many plastic valves per cycle. This was not measured.

- A new method of measurement was implemented which effectively designated the blocked off cavity as a defect.

- The measured defectives of the process, not the product, increased from 15% to 45%. A further analysis revealed the possibility that the causes of the damaged cavities could be eliminated and the overall quality improved with improved process control. The quality department was moved to the shop-floor and the operators were trained and the damaged cavities repaired.

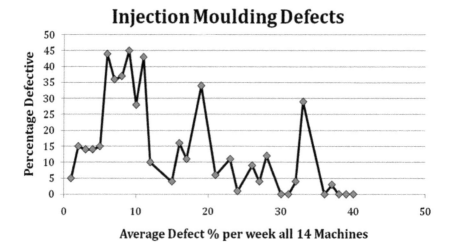

Injection Moulding Defects

Average Defect % per week all 14 Machines

Figure 8.1 Precision Valve Australia.

- 40 weeks later, the defect rate was almost zero and the productivity had doubled and it was no longer necessary to buy 14 new injection moulding machines.

- It is useful to record the achievement under our thesis, of people, process and precision.

People

Prior to this work, the Management Team believed that the machines were working at approximately 95% to 99%. The real productivity was 55% and management were not aware of it – they had lost touch with the shop-floor. The instant reaction of the Operations Director, Dr. Bob Blake, was disbelief. The organisation structure and reporting system had failed. A strong bond developed between people in the project and the net result was the elevation of good performers, recognition of achievements by the operators, and a strong desire to improve.

Process

The process was documented to ensure that the PDCA and SDCA wheels of Kaizen improvement were in place. SPC techniques were taught and applied, and the company began exporting to Japan, Singapore, New Zealand and Germany and a limited amount to the USA.

Precision

The key to the improvement process was taking meaningful measurements. The change did not finish there as the company began to aim for Six Sigma processes.

8.2 Pirelli Cables

(*Permission by Dr. Ezzelino Leonardi, Technical Director, Pirelli.*)

Once again, the 12-Step Implementation Plan was used. The Executive Team identified four projects as being critical to increasing productivity:

- Reduction in breakdowns of machinery
- Reduction in labour turnover
- Improved extrusion
- Improved wire drawing

Teams were trained in the basics of data collection using run charts, checksheets and histograms, and simple cause and effect analysis using Ishikawa charts. After the first six months, no great improvement had been recorded but a slight improvement in the attitude of the operators had been noticed. Pirelli stuck with the program.

Improvements were visible especially with a significant reduction in major defects and major breakdowns. Before the project began, the quality manager showed me a graph of the major defects for the plant from the time it was built to the day our program started. The graph showed an inexorable decrease in quality and a continuous loss in productivity. In eight months, this had been reversed. As shown in Figure 8.2, the project continued for three years and the productivity doubled and the major defect rate was reduced from 200 to 20.

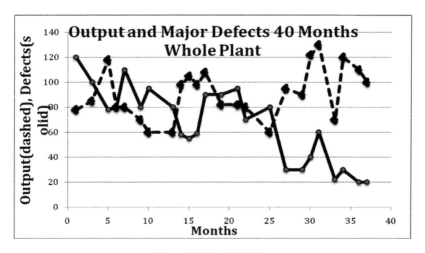

Figure 8.2 Pirelli Cables.

People

The labour turnover at the beginning of the project was reduced from 45% to 10% over the three years. At the beginning of the project, labour was moving from Pirelli to the opposition. After 2.5 years, this was reversed and the labour was moving from the opposition to Pirelli.

Process

The philosophy of breakdown maintenance had changed from breakdown to prevention. Control charts were introduced and further improvements were recorded. Pirelli was well on its way to at least a Three Sigma or Four Sigma company when the consulting program ended and Pirelli believed they had enough skills to go it alone. Near the end, the program was introduced to the Accounts Department to enable the CEO to have more accurate data produced quickly for the owners in Milan. This was achieved and Pirelli Sydney moved from Number 12 on the international totem pole of performance to Number 2 behind the main Italian factory. The last project was the successful implementation of IT internal process into cable manufacture using many of the 26 Rules for Lean Systems.

Precision

The HR processes of hiring and training had improved dramatically whilst the use of control charts had lifted the level of quality to a new level of reliability and perfection.

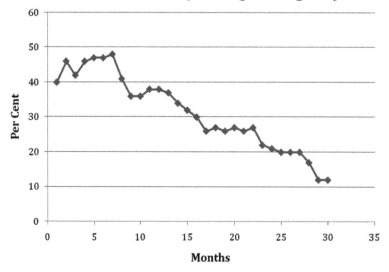

Figure 8.3 Labour turnover at Pirelli.

8.3   Geelong Cement Adelaide Brighton

(Permission by Mr. Richard Hammond, Adelaide Brighton.)

Geelong Cement had significant productivity problems and was threatened with closure. The 12-Step Implementation Plan was introduced and teams trained in key areas:

- The quarry
- Cement kilns
- Waste reduction generally
- Customer feedback
- Finishing

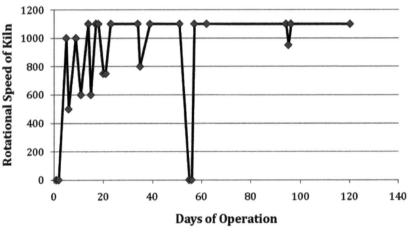

Productivity Gains Cement Kiln

Figure 8.4 Improvement in kiln output (average speed correlates with productivity).

The overall improvement in reducing the variability of the feed from the quarry to the kiln resulted in less tampering of the kiln controls and enabled an improvement in the measuring technique and so stop many kiln slowdowns. This had been the major cause of low productivity. The kiln slowdowns were a good illustration of the combination of two factors affecting productivity, namely, what Dr. Deming calls tampering and the effect of large variation in the quality of the input. By working with the teams we were able to reduce the kiln slowdowns and the massive improvement in quality and productivity followed.

People

The general culture at Geelong Cement at the start of the program was, unlike Pirelli, good. Gary Lingford ably led the teams and the Seven Steps to System Improvement chart was introduced and the people trained, the improvement began to flow fairly quickly. Richard Hammond was very impressed. A further culture improvement followed.

Process

As mentioned, this was a good example of how reducing variability and eliminating tampering can improve quality and productivity relatively quickly.

Precision

Overall, the technology was old, but the life of the plant was extended significantly.

8.4   Silver Soldering Defects and the Purchasing Manager

I hold a patent in liquid metal transfer, so I know a little about silver soldering. The solution to the high defect rate was clear from day one but the operators and management had to believe it and own the new method. I approached the purchasing manager with the idea that the supplier of the raw materials for the soldering process should be invited in to address the operators with the best way to solder. The purchasing manager saw this as interference and would not support the suggestion. I then asked all the operators to write down what their method was since there was no reasonable quality system in place. All were different. Discussion followed and general principles were taught. Finally a new method was agreed and introduced and the operators shared knowledge through the team meetings. The results are illustrated in Figure 8.5. In 28 days the defects were eliminated.

People

The lack of support by the purchasing manager was circumvented. In the future this role must become one of supply chain management.

Process

The new method was given to the quality department. At the same time the quality department was investigating a problem of collapsed foam after the product had been sold in the USA. They spent a lot of time investigating the effect of temperature on the brittleness of the foam in an attempt to solve the problem without success. When the team I formed investigated the process of making the foam I asked for a drawing of the process for mixing the chemicals to make the polyurethane foam. I was told it was Italian and therefore of no value.

I insisted and discovered that the hole controlling the mixing pressure in the busselletta bush, was absent. The two chemicals forming the foam were therefore not mixed in the correct proportion. The bush had been replaced sometime earlier and the company did not make the part with the hole. The hole was reinstated and the collapsed foam problem disappeared.

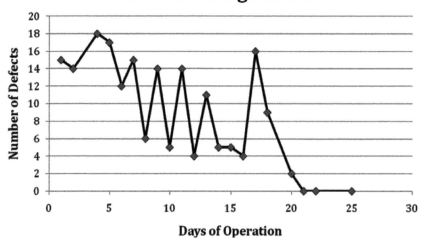

Figure 8.5 Removal of silver soldering defects.

Precision

The company in many other areas had a long way to go. Other projects in the bottleneck area of the paint-line, increased the productivity of the whole plant by 5% in six months – for 1,750 people, this was significant.

8.5   Colour Matching in Leather, Austanners

(*Dennis Thams of Austanners gave permission to use this data.*)

Colour matching in a cow-hide was believed to be an insoluble problem until the scientific method was introduced. The results, as illustrated in Figure 8.6, were spectacular. The teams in this company worked extremely well under the able leadership of Dennis Thams.

People

Excellent leadership combined with adequate training in the seven tools and some of the 26 Rules for Lean Systems resulted in a cooperative culture and this led to significant productivity improvements.

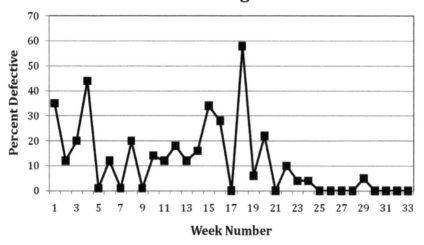

Figure 8.6 100-year-old problem.

8.6 Acceleration of the Internal Supply Chain at Shaw, December 1999 to February 2003

(*All results here are reproduced from the Initial Public Offering.*)

Over the 2.7 years of my involvement, a slight loss of $0.5 million was converted to a profit of $40 million EBITA at the same time as working capital was reduced by $40 million and on-time deliveries improved from 32.7% to approximately 95 to 99%. The profit results are shown in Figure 8.7. The 26 Rules for Lean Systems and the 22 Creative Ideas for Innovation had worked extremely well.

Earnings Before Interest Tax Amortisation Shaw Feltex

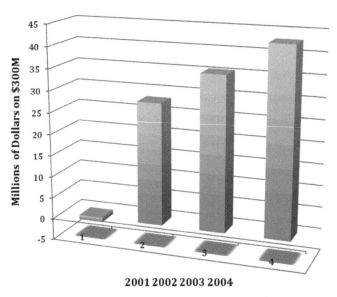

2001 2002 2003 2004

Figure 8.7 Increased profit at Shaw/Feltex (see Feltex Initial Public Offering).

8.7 The Creative Innovative Company Program (CICP) for Small Companies

(*All companies gave permission to use this data.*)

This is an extract from the final report of the CICP, which has been implemented in seven small companies in Tasmania, using the innovative methodology developed and successfully implemented in a $300 million per year turnover company.

CICP using lean to achieve high velocity

The three main causes of business failure are under-capitalisation, poor operational effectiveness and poor business planning. Business planning in the context of this program consists of strategic planning and operational planning and formulating a guide to the use of creative flow techniques to improve profitability. It is about opportunities and competitive positioning and about operational effectiveness. It improves the business using:

- Strategic planning guides
- 26 Rules for Lean Systems
- 22 Creative Ideas for Innovation
- Seven Steps to System Improvement (scientific method)

The objective of this program was to illustrate the advantage of a significant development of the Toyota production system and the Honda Best Product Program when it is applied to small business with a wide range of products or short production runs. SME business owners are not used to thinking strategically about their business. Using the 26 Rules for Lean Systems involves strategic thinking and therefore involves thinking 'outside the square'.

Measurements must be accurate and timely, representative and relevant. To understand the strategic positioning of a business it is necessary to understand the competitive nature of the business in the market. The strategic plan should overlay all operational plans. Successful strategic plans must have the ability to increase value to customers and improve the competitive position.

High-quality will always remain as a competitive advantage. However, in future, Australia businesses will need to be focussed on knowledge, human skills, logistics capabilities, creative value-added flow and clever data interpretation.

The initial plan for this project was to run ten workshops. This was exceeded since the participants needed more training than initially planned. Two delegates, plus two observers, were allowed from each company, with representatives from the

Department of Economic Development, the Manufacturing Society of Australia and Technical and Further Education organisations. The number of people participating back at the company depended on the size of the company.

As was anticipated, the measuring systems in small companies needed to be extensively modified and improved for the full benefits of the company to be realised. There was a significant need for process innovation in all of the participating companies.

Participants

- Novaris Pty. Ltd, Kingston
- Uniform City, Hobart
- Tasmanian Timber Engineering, Cambridge
- SERS, South Burnie
- AMAX Engineering Pty. Ltd, Rocherlea
- Hazard Systems Pty. Ltd, Launceston
- Muir Engineering, Kingston
- Technical and Further Education Clarence Campus
- Skilled Engineering
- Manufacturing Society of Australia
- Department of Economic Development

Measurements, the core objectives and principles applied to a range of companies.

General outcomes of the program

The feedback at the end of the first workshop was positive and participants were committed to make the program work. The main objective of this program is to see if the simpler version of the 26 Rules for Lean Systems and their application can improve the SMEs, as much as it has in the larger companies. All companies participated well although the rate of progress was variable.

Muir Engineering

This company achieved a significant improvement in profitability and inventory was reduced. Despite some drawbacks, the program succeeded. There is a strong recognition now that if Muir is going to succeed in Europe and the USA and compete with China, it must implement more flexible systems with a supply chain with a rapid service response. The ZARA International model is highly relevant. Main achievements were improved profitability, reduced working capital, reduced inventory and recognition of a need to rationalise product components and outsource more. Muir has recently won numerous Australian Government export awards.

AMAX Engineering

AMAX Engineering has improved dramatically, particularly with the "T" screw project and the implementation of a more accurate, improved and faster financial system. General achievements were continuous flow manufacturing process, reduced time to produce financial information, a quotation system modified, flow systems studied and supply rules modified.

Hazard Systems

Hazard Systems has made significant improvements to productivity, plant layout, and supply and inventory control. Control of printed circuit board supply has removed a bottleneck. Sales are increasing, but there is now pressure on space and labour skills. Significant outcomes were elimination of most back orders, new plant layout with continuous flow design, main sub-contractor control improved, and improved order system with major production increase. These improvements have resulted in an approximate 200% productivity gain. Hazard Systems are now able to accept orders two-to-three times larger than before with the same staff levels.

Novaris

Novaris improved methods of raw materials supply have reduced the lead-time and improved workflow. Other changes were an improved ordering system resulting in significantly reduced inventory and improved customer service.

Tasmanian Timber Engineering

A continuous flow model was developed for the whole of the manufacturing process. To realise the full potential, a significant capital injection is required. A new truss plant has been designed. Main outcomes are improved rationalisation of product planning and scheduling and a new plant concept agreed.

Uniform City

Raw materials control and batch sizes as well as sequencing and customer liaison have all improved. Processes and systems still need improvement. Waste has been reduced and OH&S problems were solved. A new flow production line has been designed and is to be installed. The company has now designed and implemented a completely new production line with significant financial investment.

SERS

The major achievements were working towards a new plant layout, improving value-added and improving the financial system. Expansion plans are well under way.

TAFE

The full report also includes substantial feedback from TAFE participants, with an emphasis on their learning achievements as far as business practices and recognition of a need for improved culture and capability in our Manufacturing Industries.

8.8 Conclusions

The most significant characteristic of all seven small businesses in this program is the need to understand process innovation. They operate in a market where their market-share is very small, but their systems and equipment and use of IT software needs improvement. They do not fully understand process innovation. They do not need new products at their present stage of development in the majority of cases. There is no point in introducing new products if the company cannot make them at a competitive price and quality.

The most significant achievements so far are:

- Hazard Systems increased productivity by over 200%.
- Uniform City has now implemented a completely new production system based on continuous flow.
- Timber Engineering has conceptually designed a new flow production system.

- The additive sum of the improvement in profitability for all these small companies is in excess of $2.5 million where the sum of the turnovers was approximately only $20 million.

Chapter 9

Fast Future

Summary

With the increased emphasis on personalisation of all services the demands on the business will intensify and this further emphasises the need for the business to apply all the tools of the fourth industrial revolution and beyond.

9.1 Introduction

Our fast future is about fast research and development, fast innovation of process and product, fast movement of products, and fast service using the enablers of the Industry 4.0 revolution. This involves the integration of technological advances with our human ability to see the opportunities it creates and to educate the enablers to achieve maximum competitive advantage. Also involved is the compression of the time taken to travel along the supply chain. As well, there needs to be fast integration and the speed of the available information needed for accurate and precise decision-making.

Digital data and new technologies already make much of this possible. The silicon chip computers have reached their zenith and will soon be replaced by quantum computers. Perhaps we will soon be able to tap the surface energy of metals for previously

Technology for Business: Application of the Advances in Industry 4.0 to Small to Medium Sized Enterprises
John Blakemore
Copyright © 2023 Jenny Stanford Publishing Pte. Ltd.
ISBN 978-981-4968-70-6 (Hardcover), 978-1-003-38216-4 (eBook)
www.jennystanford.com

unheard of or unimagined precision, speed and miniaturisation. Globalisation and the speed of the micro-processor are already accelerating the rate of change of business as never before. As the world suddenly expands from nation state to global village; the electron shatters trade and commercial barriers. The resulting revolution in data-interchange and knowledge has increased the speed of supply chains to the customer and the flow of capital between the links. It has also, however, increased the complexity of decision-making and magnified the risk of errors.

To combat this, business leadership will need to be more creative, more skilled and capitalise on mind capital. We are entering the age of brain over brawn. Successful businesses of the future will quickly separate themselves from the rest as they accept the challenge of being more strategic and numerate, and employ the latest technology more quickly as they identify and create new market opportunities. In particular, new wireless and satellite technologies may render cable technology for many applications –whether copper or fibre – totally obsolete.

Massive changes are taking place in the retail and service industries. Many are now employing ideas born in manufacturing and superimposing the advantages of digitisation to the customer's advantage. Generally, the Service Industry in the supply chain has much to learn from the manufacturing industry.

Businesses must therefore monitor a larger and more complex marketplace and continuously update their technology. To do this, their internal processes must be under tighter and more predictable control with cashflow administered in real-time. It is still about, people, process and precision. Success in the future will go to those businesses that are:

- Led by an innovative CEO with good strategic and numerate skills in charge of teams of advisers with data collected precisely and immediately. Digital data in real-time.
- Using the latest technology, information and intelligence-based systems that are continuously upgraded, both in hardware and software. Much of this information has to be available to a focused workforce that is also continuously upgrading its skills.

- Mobile, using flexible operational teams and management groups continuously monitoring; not only their operational effectiveness but also shifts in the marketplace. These will be process-focused, not function-focused. Wireless technology will supply faster answers on the go.
- Teams operated by frontline staff with significant autonomy to improve service to the customer. These will be linked by wireless to the next process step.
- Structured in a tightly controlled manner and able to move quickly to take advantage of cultural and perceptive swings in the marketplace. Branding will become even more important.
- Focused on a reduced time-to-market for new products. This will quickly sort out the leaders from the followers. Such rapid product development will be linked to rapid process innovation.
- Recognise that there is a strong link between product development and innovation, and process development and innovation.

Modern technology will enable business to respond to these challenges. The problems, however, will not just be technical; they will also be cultural and new disciplines need to be learned by all. This means an increasing amount of technological and cultural change at a rapid rate. The learning organisation will replace the current conventional organisation.

Rigid functional management models fail to deal successfully with rapid technological change. This has increasingly led to the recognition that process innovation is not the sole domain of engineers and scientists, and in fact must be an inherent management skill. The computer as a driver of innovation has created significant opportunities to use innovation for growth and profit in organisations that must be regarded as akin to a living organism.

The future of business lies with accelerated supply chains in product, process and service development. The focus must be on the value-added steps in innovation and elimination of the non-value-added ones. It is essential to have continuous feedback to all processes to reduce the time-to-market for new ideas, new products, new services and new ways to market them. Branding will continue to grow in significance as a way to the hearts and wallets of the consumer.

Innovation will saturate the strategic plan for all processes. In essence, this means that product and services innovation will be interwoven with process innovation and to everyone's job function. There is an increasing recognition that passing costs, waste and delays, upstream and downstream in a supply chain, helps nobody.

World-wide, leading manufacturers are finding that it may be necessary to actually build their own production equipment to achieve greater flexibility in satisfying customer needs.

Nowhere is this more noticeable than at Honda. This strong link between marketing strategy and production capability and design can lead to significant strategic advantages when these are linked to SPEED teams for innovation. A more detailed discussion of SPEED teams is available on www.blakemore.com.au.

Global business in the future will be more competitive than ever before, and the winners will be those that grab the innovation advantage of the inherent creativity of all their employees and recognise that operational processes – including research and development – must be controlled and strongly customer-focused. It is about velocity.

9.2   Enabling Technologies for a Fast Future

The Scientific American published an excellent volume on future technologies in the volume "Key Technologies for the 21st Century". This summary is now a little dated but still very valuable. What follows is my attempt to bring this up to date and focus the discussion on the theme of this book for business. I accept responsibility for this re-interpretation of the article and hope it is viewed in good faith. This was also presented earlier in the Australian Graduate School of Engineering Publication.

Information technology

Micro-processors are now doubling in speed every 1.5 years. In fact, their performance has improved by 25,000 times in less than 25 years. They have not only become faster; they have also become smaller and cheaper. This trend will continue but the limit for the silicon micro-chip has almost been reached.

Micro-processors are now three times faster than had been predicted in the early 80s. This defies some of the normal laws of innovation, prediction and forecasting. Part of the reason is a key technique that the Scientific American calls called pipelining. Pipelining is the integration of process steps. It is analogous to changing a fragmented manufacturing system into a continuous flow system. The lean manufacturing methods developed in Japan in the 80s similar to the Fuji-Xerox plant I visited in 1985, involved all assembling on a moving conveyor as an early example of this.

As discussed in the Scientific American, improvements in processing chips are ineffectual unless they are matched by similar gains in memory chips. The capacity of Random Access Memory (RAM) has increased fourfold every three years, but memory speed has not been able to keep up. The gap between the top speed of processors and the top speed of memories is widening.

However, computing methodology can be revised suddenly by some strategic chaotic input. It is believed that pipelining, superscalar processing and caches will continue to play an important part in the advancement of micro-processor technology. These micro-processors will be appearing in practically everything that is technological. When this is combined with advances in sensorisation and miniaturisation of components we see we are rapidly entering the world of Dick Tracey's wrist radio. The range of applications will be mind boggling. They will involve voice recognition, virtual reality, light switches, even pieces of paper. Perhaps combined with biomimicry and photovoltaic technologies, we will have roof tiles able to generate electricity. Just imagine the manufacturing and service applications for such technology and the effect it will have. In addition, it is possible in the future that micro-processor memory could merge and blend.

However, here lies the risk. If quality is not at the Six Sigma level, problems like that on the Qantas Airbus or locked cruise control systems reported on some Ford 4WD and locked

Electronic Stability Programs on the Citroen can possibly cause loss of life. In fact, Audi, with their Audi TT, suffered the indignity of not solving the massive computer programming error in their 4WD version and instead it was up to a team of British scientists to solve this problem. 14 people were killed on the autobahn. Audi thought they could solve the problem by using rollover protective bars in the cabin. Such a solution is reactive and after the event, not preventive.

Artificial intelligence (AI)

The computer has shown already that many actions we think are difficult can be readily automated and sped up. Many of the tasks that are easy for people to do cannot be done successfully by computers at present. Massive advances have been made as illustrated by Honda's ASIMO robot and the associated health and age-related devices as spinoffs. ASIMO Robot: A Simulated Mobility Robot, built by the Honda Motor Company walks like a man. The spinoff from this has already been significant, particularly for devices for elderly people.

Computerised reasoning has very narrow strength and wide weaknesses. As well, predictions of achievement of AI have been overly optimistic. Some people now believe that AI is on the brink of success, but given a very simple problem that is beyond the expertise of the programming, ridiculous answers can turn up.

The process of knowledge-interchange between people cannot currently be automated. One can postulate that part of the problem with such AI programs is the multiple meaning of words. This in turn could ultimately dilute our language. The programs have to understand the natural languages and employ an existing knowledge-base to comprehend a wide variety of texts, which can be laden with ambiguity, metaphor and sarcasm. The processors can check grammar and spelling, but what about intonation, double meanings and honesty? Already this causes significant errors when texting. If this system is going to work it could be that we are on the verge of a more rational, universal language based on truth and a computer conversant only with intelligent software. Julian Assange would be pleased.

As palm top diaries, smart cards and interactive television proliferate, the gap between users and non-users will probably become even more noticeable. More and more people are spending more time in front of television sets and computer screens collecting, assimilating, visually assessing complex collections of software information. The digital world is dictating our behaviour.

Software agents (programs) have been born. These know the users interests and can act autonomously on their behalf. There will be no secrets. Once you access a program or site on the Internet, your identity will be known. Such programs differ from regular software programs, by seeing themselves as separate entities. Agents will learn by experience to be flexible and adaptive and will respond to unforeseen circumstances, as well as being multi-tasked. Everyone will have to be more truthful. People have been trying to build on such knowledge-based agents for over 40 years, but now it appears that they could be on the verge of success. In the future, as external demands for information alter, the software system itself will continually renew itself. The social impact of this will be enormous. We ignore these issues at our peril.

Virtual reality

Computers are already becoming extensions of our bodies. This permits everyone to behave as if they were somewhere else. This place may be fiction or a recreated environment from another place or another time. Scientists are making significant progress with tele-transportation. Michio Kaku in "Parallel Worlds: The Science of Alternative Universes and our Future in the Cosmos" is serious about the multiverse.

Virtual reality transports perceptions by appealing to all our major senses, sight, hearing and touch at the same time and by presenting images that respond immediately to one's movements. Head-mounted stereoscopic displays used in virtual reality will be replaced soon by lightweight glasses that can superimpose images on the real world. It will be possible to simultaneously use a large number of perceptive skills to interpret information for the first time. Virtual reality will make little distinction between body and mind.

Where will this lead and what are the implications for business? New instruments for measuring human perceptions will be born and our behaviour will be observed in real-time.

There will be no secrets. Business and big brother will know all about us. People moving past us in a crowd can scan our wallet and pick up our credit card details in them instantaneously.

Satellites and wireless technologies

Satellites in the future will provide almost universal access to the information in cyberspace. Solid copper wire or fibre connections will become old hat. Satellite systems will soon bring communication to the half of the world's population that is currently hours travelling time from the nearest phone. Doctors and other specialists in these areas will have immediate access to the best information and the best people around the world. What a revolution! Suddenly there will be an explosion of awareness. We will have the benefit of all available knowledge at the speed of light.

A probable most important consequence of satellite communications may be that it will help to stem the large scale of migration of people from the countryside to cities and densely populated urban areas. There will be a redistribution of population.

Technology blending

The blending of the basic digital technology of the computer with the television has already begun. This will mean that the differentiation between computer and television set will become increasingly blurred until they will merge into one.

9.3   Environment and Technologies

Michio Kaku claims that we only have 400 years of conventional energy, coal oil, gas and uranium left. Alternatives must be found quickly. The waste-makers of society must be tackled right at the fundamentals of generation of industrial, agricultural and energy waste. This means more recycling, more re-use and smarter use of what is almost freely available – sunlight, sea, wind and tide.

Solar power

The earth receives ten times as much energy from sunlight as is contained in all of the known reserves of uranium, oil, natural gas and coal. Despite confusion created by people like Tim Flannery in "Weathermakers", the sun is the most important determinant of weather. We do live in a goldilocks time where even the rotation of the moon orbiting the earth is synchronised with the earth's rotation, and we only ever see one side of the moon.

Since 1861, people have been trying to effectively harness solar power. The beneficial effect of the use of solar energy in reducing air pollution and global climatic change is well-documented. It is highly unlikely that a single solar technology will predominate. Electric power can be generated by:

- Building solar heat engines
- Photovoltaic cells
- Harnessing the power of rivers and dams
- Burning bio-mass
- Erecting wind turbines
- Bio-mass fuel, such as ethanol and methanol
- Methane technologies
- Fuel cells
- Fossil fuels like coal, and gas
- Nuclear fission
- Nuclear fusion
- Ammonia technologies

Whilst only a miniscule amount of the available energy is converted into wind power, it is still significant in terms of energy consumption by people. It is hoped that solar technologies will enable the developing world to skip a generation of energy production infrastructure.

Exciting prospects are emerging whereby roof coatings are being developed that have photovoltaic properties.

Green energy from hydrogen

Renewables used to produce hydrogen for all forms of energy but not particularly transportation.

Fusion

Work in France is continuing with the International Thermal Energy Reactor (ITER). This is a slow and very expensive process for so far no commercial outcomes.

It has been one of man's most recent dreams to recreate nuclear fusion. Fusion uses atoms present in ordinary water as a fuel and harnessing this process could ensure future generations of adequate electric power. Fusion has so far failed to deliver. The problem is basically containment of the reaction. The containment of the plasma is a balanced magnetic field. The larger the reactor the more stable the plasma. ITER reactors are likely to be large and very expensive. If the containment problem can be solved, then our future energy problems would be removed.

The future of agriculture

The farmer has to go high-tech. Technology has been the most reliable force in increasing farm productivity. It must be sustainable. Integrated pest management systems are being used to control the harvest. This is a result of pooling and interpretation of a vast body of knowledge of insect biology. "Biomimicry, Innovation Inspired by Nature" by Janine Benyus explains this elegantly and in significant detail.

Knowledge of nature is being used to design new products. Corn starch plastic will replace polyethylene for many applications. As this knowledge increases, more and more clever inventions will be harnessed to increase productivity. New farm implements for agriculture will also be used to great effect.

Materials, manufacturing, machines

The future of machines, materials and manufacturing will involve:

- Increased use of robotics
- Microscopic machines
- The use of advanced composites and intelligent materials and self-assembling materials
- Custom manufacturing in higher temperature, super-conductors
- Highly versatile and flexible integrated machinery

Robots

Currently, it is believed that the first robot went into production in 1961 in a die-casting operation. Now there are millions of robots operating world-wide. Some people forecast that homes of the future will involve automation systems that will outlive the occupants. Others envisage that robots will serve and mix with humans for everlasting mutual benefit.

One of the most important lessons learned so far about robotics is that they can only be used in systems that are operating under tight control. If the system they automate is poor then the product is still poor. The human skill in handling the development of robots may well determine the levels of human activity in the next century. The ASIMO robot can walk like a human.

Microscopic machines

New electronic fabrication processes can currently produce such things as data storage chips or even a chemical factory on a micro-chip. Researchers in micro-electronics have already built motors that can be deployed to move atoms. These are only microns in size (one micron is one thousandth of a millimetre). Micro-mechanical devices of the future will supply electronic systems with a window to the physical world which will enable us to use all of our senses. The advances in technology and technical peripherals will be enormous as we couple mechanical and electronic micro-systems. A library of information will be written in an area the size of a micro-chip. Arrays of micro-valves will release drug doses into bloodstreams at precisely timed intervals. For this to work the process must be controlled precisely, people, process and precision must be as one. Where is the limit? I already have two acrylic lens implants that are superior to the lenses Mother Nature gave me.

Micro-electro mechanical systems

Micro-electro mechanical systems have already been born. Engineering of small machines and sensors will allow new uses for conventional ideas. These systems will give micro-electronics an opening to the world beyond simply processing and storing information. Imagine a chemical factory on a chip. Such a calculator size device could reconstitute freeze-dried drugs and perform DNA testing. The world will be very, very, different.

Advanced composites

Much of the promise of advanced composites in providing greater strength, lower weight and hence greater fuel efficiency for moving vehicles has been realised. Carbon fibre composites are revolutionising air travel and yacht design, and as the price comes down more and more applications will emerge. This will greatly reduce transport costs.

Will it be possible to combine carbon with ceramics and so enable say internal combustion engines to operate at higher temperatures and greater efficiencies with automotive bodies much lighter that steel and aluminium? The fracture and sinking of the America's Cup yacht 'One Australia' is evidence of how little is known about the real performance of some of these materials at that time. While we have moved on since then catastrophic failures of say yacht spars are not that uncommon. Much is yet to be done, but where will it lead when these problems are solved?

Intelligent materials

Scientists are now creating materials that can predict failure and repair themselves and materials that can adapt to the environment in which they are being used. Biomimicry is real.

Imagine buildings that reinforce themselves during an earthquake. Many researchers have already demonstrated the feasibility of such living materials. Steel 'work hardens', but little use has so far been made of this. In fact, as the dislocation density in steel increases the yield strength increases significantly for a penalty in ductility.

I demonstrated this commercially in 1976, but the Australian company I worked for did not go ahead because "no one else in the world is doing it". My ophthalmic surgeon said this to me in 1991 when he announced that I could go blind in 3 minutes. I suggested a scientific and engineering solution based on my 22 Creative Ideas for Innovation, and he rejected it since "no one in the world is doing this". After intense and heavy conversation over a period of time I talked him into it and my sight was saved. The 22 Creative Ideas for Innovation have served me well.

We must become leaders. All engineering structures are designed on yield data not ductility data. The skilled engineer always designs with the worst-case scenario in mind with the result the design contains very large margins of safety, redundant sub-units, numerous reinforcements and back-up systems and added weight.

Intelligent materials systems on the other hand will have great economies of scale and size. The name 'actuator' has now been given to materials that allow structures such as ladders to adapt to their environment. The four most common actuator materials are:

- Peizoelectric ceramics
- Magnetostrictive materials
- Shape memory alloys, like Nitinol
- Electro-rheological and magneto-rheological fluids

These materials, such as the shape memory alloy Nitinol, have outstanding characteristics but are only just being understood. Use of such materials will release a brand new way of engineering. Such materials will be able to sense their environment, store detailed information and experiment. The most lasting influence will be on the philosophy of design. This advance may eliminate catastrophic failures forever. Applications for forecasting are mind boggling.

Self-assembling materials

Complex machines of the future cannot be built with current methods. It will be necessary for them to almost make themselves. Self-Assembled Monolayers (SAMs) are a simple prototype that exemplifies the design principles that people are investigating with self-assembling materials. The result of understanding how this work will enable such things as placement of the silicon and doping atoms in the semi-conductor crystal to be done by the materials themselves, not by individual human intervention.

Nature abounds with examples of self-assembly. Consider a raindrop on a leaf. The raindrop assumes the shape required for an optical lens. Nature creates magic all around us. Self-assembling materials are about using nature in manufacture.

Superconductivity

Superconductivity may be regarded as the path of zero resistance. It is well known that the path of least resistance is the one that nature prefers, but such a path is not always readily revealed. It is why a yacht can plane and stop pushing water and instead skip over the top.

When superconductivity was discovered in 1911 with liquid helium at 4 Kelvin (4 degrees above absolute zero). It was observed that mercury would suddenly transmit electricity without energy loss. Superconductivity has made little advance in recent times, but is now poised to make a very significant impact on society.

In addition, what is called high temperature superconductivity has been discovered and experimented with. Such innovations will give birth to a range of supersensitive accurate and precise medical diagnostic tools like the new generation Magnetic Resonance Imaging (MRI) devices I have evaluated. The reason for this is that as experimental work goes on. The temperature at which complex materials become superconductive has continuously increased up to 93 Kelvin. Already as a result of superconducting research, superconducting quantum interference devices can serve as a highly sensitive detector of magnetic fields and as such can detect weak magnetic signals from the heart and brain. This opens up a brand new area of scientific investigation and previously unimagined medical benefits.

New superconducting materials could probably boost the speed of computation by another fifty times. Once superconductivity is better understood higher and higher transition temperatures may be reached, but already we have Maglev. This high-speed train relies on superconductivity to levitate.

9.4   Medicine

Surgeons of the future will be like engineers. Much of the surgery will be done robotically with a far greater precision than in the past.

The 21st Century will see innovative solutions to some of the world's most important medical problems. This will involve greater use of artificial organs, gene therapy, improved methods of prediction of disease and medical history forecasts from blood samples. Gene therapy will allow doctors to treat many diseases by injecting needed genes directly into the blood stream. This is already being used for treating disease such as several combined immuno deficiencies. Other diseases to be treated in clinical trials on gene therapy are cancer, AIDS, arthritis, peripheral vascular disease, haemophilia and cystic fibrosis.

Artificial organs

Already, medical science has moved beyond the practice of transplantation into the area of manufacture and fabrication. The idea is to make organs rather than simply to move them from donor to recipient. Artificial plastic tissues have already been created and genetic engineering may soon produce universal donor cells, cells that do not provoke rejection by the immune system, whilst the transference of organs from animals may overcome the shortage of organs.

The future will also involve using ultra pure biodegradable plastics and polymers as substrates for cell culture, implantation and generation of tissue. Using computer-aided design scientists and engineers will be able to manufacture plastics into beds that mimic the structure of specific tissues and even organs and these scaffolds will be treated with compounds that help cells to adhere.

9.5   Logistics and Transportation

Some of the immediate advances in this area will range from magnetically levitated high-speed rail, huge single wing flying aircraft, driverless cars and tiny spacecraft. These are just some of the future technologies that are now in store for us. The built-in intelligence in automobiles will enable the drivers to tune themselves into the situation and so navigate through crowded traffic systems faster and safer. If high-quality is abandoned, the risks will increase. Japan is already experimenting with trains that can reach 650 km/h.

Advances in materials and design will translate into cheaper and safer air travel. It is believed unlikely in the near future this will be very much faster than it is today. The emphasis will be on safety and size, but very fast rail traffic will become a very serious competitor to not only the motor-car but the plane as well. This is already the case with Maglev trains on the drawing board in China.

The ability of man to adapt to change has always been a problem. However, the rate of technological change today is increasing continuously and this change is a result of the scientific method and the inherent ability of scientific process to build on firm foundations. Human elements dominate other areas of society to a larger degree than scientific research but as we have seen with the climate change and greenhouse gas debate and the role of the Inter-Government Panel on Climate Change (IPCC), the human element can give rise to irrational exuberance. Hence, scientific arguments do not appear to apply to the same degree to social development, politics and – in some cases – human resource development.

The difference between change in the past and change now, is that now we have many of the tools to deal with it. Globalisation is firmly telling us that the status quo, particularly in Australia, is not good enough. In addition, as more and more of the 220 countries in the world become liberal democracies, the rules for business are starting to equilibrate. The principles underlying the liberal democratic process will in future have more and more influence on the overall principles of business management.

9.6   Innovation the Way Forward

If we look at the commercialisation of innovation, the gap between invention and payback is narrowing distinctly. In 1666, it took the world 27 years to simply know that Isaac Newton had developed the theory of calculus (Table 9.1). Newton was so afraid to release it that he hid it in a drawer and was only forced to reveal it when another mathematician in Germany also developed it and the two had to be separated by a challenge in problem-solving laid down by the Royal Society.

Table 9.1 Commercialisation of innovation

Year	Average time from discovery to use
1666	27 years for Isaac Newton to publish calculus
1880	30 years
1945	16 years
1967	9 years
1985	2 years
2020	?

In 1880, the commercialisation of inventions was still taking 30 years, whilst in 1967 it had been reduced to nine years. In 1985, this was reduced to two years. In the year 2020, how long will it take? Mark Zuckerberg found his ideas in the marketplace in Facebook fairly quickly but how long will it take to commercialise the ITER reactor (fusion reactor), if it ever works?

In the future, the ability of business to grow will depend increasingly on its ability to innovate and create and drive the market. Companies are already using innovation and change management as a strategic weapon. The best early illustration of this was the Honda-Yamaha war in Tokyo in the mid-80s. Yamaha claimed that they were the foremost motorcycle manufacturer in the world and Honda responded by introducing a plethora of new models, demolishing the market for Yamaha and leaving massive stocks of unsold motorcycles in the Yamaha showrooms. Yamaha surrendered.

The SPEED teams used by Honda in this creative surge were cross-functional and linked to Sales (S), Production (P), Engineering (E) and Development (D). These teams could innovate more quickly because of Honda's very strong Formula 1 experiences. However, these processes must be done with Six Sigma precision. Six Sigma at 3 ppm is off the normal distribution chart as shown in Figure 9.1.

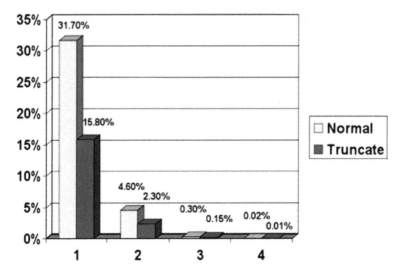

Figure 9.1 Quality defective % versus Sigma. Six Sigma is off the graph. The truncated bars are for hospitals.

If the major elements of change in business today are analysed and prioritised, it would be possible to get a list of the top ten as shown in Table 9.2. This is an adaptation of the table prepared by Freddie Soon of the Singapore Productivity Council in his publication "Asia Pacific Service and Quality Conference".

Table 9.2 Global competitiveness – networks

1.	Globalisation
2.	Technological explosion
3.	International consumerism
4.	Brain not labour
5.	Systematic networks
6.	Electronic databases/data-interchange
7.	Shift to Asia
8.	Triumph of fact over fiction
9.	Supremacy of knowledge-based decision-making
10.	Team creativity

Note: This list could be expanded with lower priority items.

For companies to be successful in the global marketplace, they must be equipped to be able to respond quickly to changes in perceptions of the customer. The change in the company itself must be able to respond to chaotic inputs. Quality and subsequent internal business systems must be under tight control. If this is so, the company can be highly flexible and respond quickly to massive input changes. To cope with this, companies are increasingly building networks with specialised suppliers. When taken to the extreme, some people say that Toyota is not a manufacturer, it is designer and an assembler.

To focus on increasing velocity, global companies are outsourcing as shown in Table 9.3, which is a good example of the globalisation of business and the dissolution of the nation state. For the Pontiac Le Mans, GM in USA is outsourcing most of its components depending on the best and most successful supplier – is it an American car?

Table 9.3 Globalisation of business – dissolution of the nation state

1.	For a Pontiac Le Mans – GM
2.	South Korea for routine labour and assembly
3.	Japan for advanced components
4.	Germany for styling and design engineering
5.	Taiwan, Singapore and Japan for small components
6.	Britain for advertising and marketing
7.	Ireland, Barbados for data processing

Rapid change in commercialisation and electronic data-interchange puts greater emphasis on companies to be globally competitive. The Singapore Productivity Board has attempted to measure global competitiveness using the following measures.

- Openness
- Government
- Finance
- Labour
- Infrastructure
- Technology

- Management
- Civil institutions
- Legal framework
- Productivity
- Technical skill
- Worker attitude
- Labour force evaluation measure

Presumably innovation is there somewhere, but where? In my view, global competitiveness is about innovation to create a competitive advantage.

Business is a complex mixture of all skills. The secret for business success in the future will be even more closely tied to digital data and our human ability to use it and then think outside the square. Some of the immediately observable technological changes we see around us are:

- POS technology in real-time
- Supply chain integration
- Flatter organisational structures
- Digital ordering and information availability
- Technology at the customer interface to make the customer work at the POS – the petrol station is a good example

The consumer is well aware of the increased utilisation of electronic data-interchange for process control in the Service Industry, in particular; for example, POS technology. The technology is already available to us for electronically updating stock and control and placing orders direct on manufacturers. This reduces the number of steps in the supply chain, increases speed, decreases inventory and decreases waste. Such improvements in efficiency are even amplified on the World Wide Web. In addition, the effect of human error is minimised by utilising such techniques as bar coding and POS technology.

Change

The process of change could possible fit into four particular mathematical models. I believe that the four types of different relationships when taking on the big picture of business are as follows:

- Natural science – the explosion of exponential growth of knowledge
- Social development – an exponential growth, but not at the same rate as natural science
- Political development – this could be regarded as linear, zero gradient improvements are marginal
- Environmental decline – negative exponential

If the same analogy is adopted for business, the four trends are:

- Opportunities – rapid and exponential growth
- Customer-base – less rapid exponential growth
- Political will – linear zero gradient
- Competitive advantage – negative exponential if company believes its competitive advantage remains sustainable

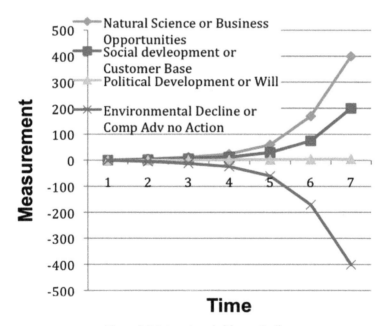

Figure 9.2 Future trends (theoretical).

Natural science and business opportunities are exponential upwards but environmental decline and a businesses competitive advantage are exponential downwards if no action taken. What this means is that we must take advantage of the latest technology, be extremely innovative and recognise opportunities or create them.

It also means that any competitive advantage of business will not remain a competitive advantage for very long because of the nature and intensity of the competition and the rapid change of technology. We therefore believe we should no longer talk of competitive advantage but instead use the SAW. Cut up your opposition with your SAW!

Already, many of the well-known global companies have seen the necessity to run tightly controlled systems, create their own opportunities or at least be aware of perceptive changes in the global market. The need to tap into world-wide process control expertise was quickly recognised by Porsche three years ago when they made a multi-billion dollar loss.

Today they are riding high – moving forward with a plethora of new models, all of them of much higher quality than ever before. How did they do it? They recognised that their major problem was one associated with quality, manufacturing techniques and innovation. They copied Japanese techniques, and introduced Kaizen and as a result they have produced new models of much higher-quality and reliability. Porsche is back.

It is all about people, process and precision ... and speed.

Action

Business can win if it takes advantage of the new opportunities created daily by new technology and new ways to configure it and then link it with people, process and precision, lean and velocity. Therefore the business approach has to change. The Board in the future, of most businesses will have to be much more strategic in its thinking and to achieve this it means that the operational aspects of the business must be under tighter control and be reported in real-time. To do this it needs knowledgeable people and the best technology.

In a nutshell, the Board must become increasingly strategic and less operational. The processes in the company must be Six Sigma – that is, zero defects – or at least 3.0 parts per million outside specification limits.

Strategic thinking is about recognising the opportunities, ensuring the correct tightly controlled processes are in place so that the Board can concentrate on the bigger tactical and strategic decisions. Business must be able to change direction and service the customer as quickly as a pit-stop in Formula 1. Big opportunities are created all around us as IT demolishes boundaries today as never before. As all countries compete on a global basis, regardless of time zones, national boundaries become irrelevant. This will eventually lead to a global rationalisation of business and political principle.

9.7 Innovation and Supply Chain Management

Accelerating the supply chain creates strategic advantages for both delivery and product and process development. Technological innovation and information technology have now multiplied the productivity of individuals thousands of times in the last two generations. On the other hand, our limited vision of the final benefits of such inventions as the transistor by William Shockley is no more evident than statements by people like Bill Gates in 1981 that '640k of memory should be enough for anybody' or IBM's CEO in 1943 who said 'the total market for computers will probably be no more than 5'. Again the statement "Nothing heavier than air can possibly fly" by the Royal Society.

The message here is that – while in hindsight it is very easy to smile at the predictions by some of the greatest minds of the century – in reality it must be recognised that our intelligence is limited and the rate of change and generation of information is so great that many do not see the potential benefits of the available technology until very late. This is the case with the technology that is currently available for supply chain integration.

As far as Australia is concerned, we have particular problems. Whilst we can all be proud of the outstanding growth rate we have been able to sustain in the last three-to-four years, and our resilience in fighting off the Asian crisis after the collapse of the Thai Baht in 1997, it is sobering to realise that the only way we have solved the chronic current account debt crisis is to be reliant on massive exports of raw materials notably coal and iron ore to China.

An area begging attention is the redesign of the supply chain. The first step is to change the mindset of our Australian companies to focus on the world market and not simply the domestic one. Whilst our larger companies are doing this, there are many that are not.

Miniature, high value-added goods can be manufactured in Australia, sold over the Internet at very high margins and quickly air-freighted to their destination anywhere in the world. How many people in Australia are doing this at the moment? How many companies have developed strategic partnerships with their customers to sell to the world?

To take advantage of the new technological opportunities, the process of supply of goods and services to the world must however be under tight control, and management must be able to use the plethora of information available. Management needs to continuously raise the bar and not simply focus on the methods of the past. The Retail Industry in particular is under serious threat and has been very slow to move. One only has to compare traditional fashion outlets with ZARA International to see the differences. Other examples are the Book Industry and the Retail Industry in general.

Strategic issues need to be linked to an improved operational effectiveness and this means that Boards must understand SPC and process integration and clearly focus on the strategies needed to improve global supply. The question now is: how do you do it?

The methods are well established and available to all of us but do not appear to be used by many. It all goes back to Dr. Ono, the Toyota, Honda, Panasonic and Canon systems and the work of Dr. Deming, Dr. Juran, Ohno, Dr. Shewhart and the Toyota and Honda production systems. Pioneers in the application of these techniques and measures have driven these companies to unprecedented levels of quality and performance in the Telecommunications and Automotive Industries world-wide. Much of this has been discussed in great detail by the US$ multi-million IMVP study of the world's Automobile Industry in the book by Jones, Roos and Womack, "The Machine that Changed the World".

So what are some of the rules that we can apply to the supply chain to create the strategic advantages of integration and reduction in lead-time? How can we improve customer relationships by delivering better and faster? These rules were introduced in Chapter 2. The objectives of supply chain integration are to supply superior quality goods faster, with more efficient processes. In essence, be more responsive to the perceptions of the marketplace and be able to change directions at will.

The major consequences of supply chain integration using, say, lean thinking techniques, originally based on TQM as expounded by Dr. Ono and Dr. Deming result in:

- Reduced inventory in the supply chain
- Reduced costs
- Faster processing speeds
- Reduced lead-times
- Reduced warehouse costs
- Reduced obsolescence
- Greater responsiveness to customers
- Electronic links to suppliers and customers
- Continuous flow of products and information
- Speeding up the development cycle
- Continuous flow, not materials and inventory overload
- Improved quality
- Happier customers

It is a sad fact in the complex business environments that exist in most small manufacturing companies with a large number of products passing through non-synchronised processes, that people think the basic rules of supply chain integration and lean manufacturing do not apply.

The 26 Rules for Lean Systems all apply to different degrees to all businesses. The application of these requires a paradigm shift in thinking. We have to be smarter; we have to respond to globalisation's new rules. Everyone in the company must contribute, everyone in the supply chain must contribute, and new ideas must be applied, tried and improved upon. We must innovate and prosper or stagnate and disappear.

All of the principles in the 26 Rules for Lean Systems are well established. I often wonder why Dr. Ono found it necessary to travel to the US and to say that the techniques he developed for Toyota resulted from the American supermarket way of doing business because the techniques were always available to him at his local sushi bar. Maybe it was his polite way of not saying that the solution was in front of us. This is illustrated in Figure 9.3.

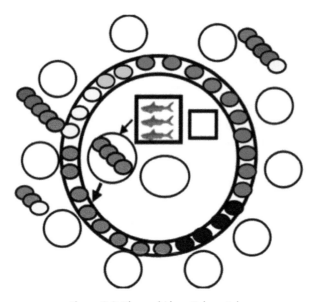

Figure 9.3 The sushi bar, Tokyo style.

When you sit at the sushi bar, as I have many times in Tokyo, you see most of what is known as the Toyota Production System in action. The inventory of seafood is only replaced when a plate is removed from the belt. The customer only eats in increments of a plate of food. The waste is almost nil since the increments are small. The cost is accurately determined by the number of plates of different colours representing the various costs of foods. The chef in the middle of the cell only cuts up fresh fish as needed. It all reflects demand. The only buffer is what is needed to speed up the process and market the product. The chef continues to polish his knife, as it is never sharp enough. It is all about people, process and precision. It is all about best practice, just-in-time and Six Sigma.

9.8 Change and the Future

The most effective way to change an organisation is to drive the change from the top but immediately engaging at all levels in the structure. This can be done with cross functional teams operating with a well-defined strategy and objective. These teams must be in areas of the business connected directly to the core processes supporting the key strategies. Once again, the basics of Quality (appropriate to customer expectations), Cost (appropriate cost aligning with key objectives), and Delivery (on time to customer expectations).

The membership of the teams must include those people who are directly involved with the process. The structure of the organisation to drive this involves the leadership by the Steering Committee. Reporting to this group are the project teams led by a team leader and facilitated either internally or externally. These teams can also involve the external customer.

For successful change to occur, the participants must be given the correct tools and techniques and access to the appropriate resources both internal and external as needed. The change process will not be quick as it involves changing people's perceptions and behaviours.

At Pirelli, in one of heir plants making cable, the steering committee identified four strategic areas for improvement all of which were aligned with the core processes of the business. These areas were:

1. The cable sheath extruder.
2. The Maintenance department.
3. Wire feed manufacture.
4. Human Resource management.

The staff turnover at the beginning of the work was 100%, i.e. in one year all the working staff would have been replaced. Three years later this was reduced to 22%. This was below the national average at the time and was still deceasing.

As mentioned, the change was not quick and only began after positive results for improvement were noticeable. In fact, in the first 6 months there was no improvement and a lot of scepticism. Morale remained low. With effective and visual leadership by the Chief Executive Officer, Mr Colin Bale, and the chief technologist, Dr. Ezzelino Leonardi, change began to occur as the processes improved. The improvement began at eight months and was very noticeable at ten months. The overall performance at the end of three years was so significant that the Pirelli's performance which was ranked at 14 out of 15 (second worst). Was lifted to 2 out of 15 and I was summoned to Milan to share ideas.

At the end of the three year long program, the output of the plant had doubled with no increase in capital expenditure. In fact, there was no need to build a second plastic feed plant.

9.9   12-Step Implementation Plan for Changing an Organisation

Step 1: Audit and training

After a brief audit, a top team, seminar was conducted. Training in the basic concepts of lean high-velocity continuous flow, was done. This was linked to the strategy and direction and future goals of the company. The training emphasised the following:

- People involvement and teamwork
- Training and learning at all levels
- Data collection, process improvement to Six Sigma
- Innovation of process and product
- The Seven Steps to System Improvement chart was used

When the basic training was complete, a plan for the introduction of process improvement teams was agreed upon. These areas were selected by the CEO and Senior Management to fit the strategic plan and reduce key bottlenecks in flow and excessive waste. In one case, all the teams were initially internal; in another, they included the supplier and another with a customer.

Step 2: Facilitator-selection and training

Three internal facilitators were selected and trained. Their task was explained as:

- Implementing the strategy
- Assisting in 'making it happen'
- Training teams in the philosophy, tools and techniques, teamwork, SPC as needed, and the identification of specialists as needed
- Identifying problems
- Encouraging change
- Planning the future by:
    - Planning progress
    - Establishing objectives
    - Formulating a timetable
    - Seeking resources
    - Formulating budgets

Step 3: Identifying pilot areas

The top team seminar identified the general area for the first set of four projects. This was further investigated and used as a starting point. (In another company, only one project was selected. This specifically had the objective of improving the quality and productivity of precision nylon parts.)

Step 4: Selection of the Steering Committee

The Steering Committee was selected by Senior Management to guide the projects. Its task also was to manage the introduction of the program. This meant:

- Leading
- Organising
- Monitoring
- Controlling
- Planning
- Allocating resources
- Communicating the program

The responsibilities of this group were:

- Setting policies and program objectives
- Establishing working committees

- Approving resources for projects
- Communicating with other parts of the organisation

Step 5: Selection of the Working Committee

In large companies, working committees are necessary. In smaller ones, they are not. In very small companies, the Executive Team may become the Project Team, as it was for the eight companies in the CICP run in Tasmania over 18 months. The membership of this committee must include the department heads covering the process (suppliers and customers), the facilitators and experts as needed (industrial engineers, statisticians, for example). The major task of the working committee is to manage the projects.

Step 6: Select and train the Project Teams

The membership of this team is determined on the basis of who can best:

- Contribute to developing the best solution.
- Ensure the effective implementation of the best solution.
- Ensure the solution remains in place.

All members were trained in the basics of process improvement data collection flowcharts and Value Stream Maps and the Seven Steps to System Improvement method.

Step 7: Identify process improvements and set standards

This step is facilitated by brainstorming by the Project Team. Problems associated with the process are identified and ranked and priorities set. A timetable for the project was set by the working committee and ratified by the Steering Committee.

Step 8: Application of the management process improvement tools

The first step in process improvement after the process has been identified is to understand the process. This is done by defining, analysing and flow-charting. Flowcharts were first macro then broken down into parts depending on what the values were based on the processes (now called "Value Stream Mapping"). When this was complete, checksheets and run charts are designed by the Project Team to measure the process. Control charts are left till much later.

Over the next few weeks, sufficient data had been collected to start identifying the areas to concentrate the improvement process and apply innovative steps. One overriding factor was obvious at this stage. The process was heavily influenced by special causes. The general flow chart on process improvement was then continued and the problems identified were ranked Pareto fashion for solution. The solution was then implemented.

Step 9: Presentation to all

The Project Team then selected a 'presenter' to celebrate the achievements gained. He was trained and the presentation to the whole of the plant carried out and recorded. (At Comalco, this was highly successful and the recording was taken around the world by the managing director, Nick Stump.)

Step 10: Cement the change in place

The objective is to make the new philosophy a way of life. This will involve changing policies and procedures, and the reporting mechanisms to reinforce the changes.

Step 11: Monitor and control the process

This involves monitoring using control charts, plotting variation limits at Three Sigma, and measuring this against the customer specification limits. When these are equal then the process has a statistical process capability of one. Later, the chairpersons are rotated to achieve continuous learning and training.

Step 12: Celebration and feedback

This involves continuous celebration of achievements and communication.

Chapter 10

Conclusion and Vision

As a consultant, the range of problems I am confronted with is extremely wide. It is this range – plus the excitement of being able to help businesses, then measure improvements – that motivates me. Whilst lean to achieve velocity is not a quick fix, many industrial processes are so far out of control (SPC) that it is prudent and sensible to introduce change in the process before control charts or even shop-floor lean techniques are introduced, and all this should be done before the full benefits of the developments and ideas and techniques of the fourth techniques can be realised.

This was the case with a large American company I worked with in 1999. The management did not understand the link between individual processes and the necessity to reduce the time between forecast and manufacture and how to link this with demand. Over-production of many products was the result and the company was so high in inventory that approximately $2.5 million of write-downs were made each year. On-time deliveries were only 33% and the customers were so unhappy that they placed orders in advance and asked the company to make and hold them before delivery. Ontime deliveries were not even measured when I started. Business has three overriding principles, QCD. Q is quality, C is cost and D is delivery. The quality must be appropriate to the demand in the first instance, but in

Technology for Business: Application of the Advances in Industry 4.0 to Small to Medium Sized Enterprises
John Blakemore
Copyright © 2023 Jenny Stanford Publishing Pte. Ltd.
ISBN 978-981-4968-70-6 (Hardcover), 978-1-003-38216-4 (eBook)
www.jennystanford.com

my experience, it has revealed that the higher the quality then the lower the cost.

The USA parent believed that the way to solve the problem was to immediately introduce lean manufacturing techniques to the shop-floor. I thought otherwise, since there was a quicker way to achieve their objectives. The management and the owners were then convinced to change the way they planned production and shorten the timeframe between demand and production by applying the 26 Rules for Lean Systems. This was only the first step. The other rules could be applied later. The audit revealed the following relationship between sales and inventory as shown in the following Figure 10.1.

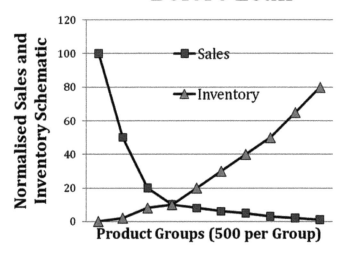

Figure 10.1 Before 26 Rules for Lean Systems.

When you analyse Figure 10.1, you wonder why anyone would continue to make those products where there is a lot of inventory and poor sales. This company had been working on removing $40 million of working capital for five years and yet could not see how to do it. When I produced the above graph and it was clear what had to be done, the next problem was to change the planning cycle. The errors created by simply forecasting from shipments, was first removed. However, this was not easy since the poor culture of the company was preventing the speed of the change needed.

The planning cycle method was then analysed, and various models considered. The product range was first stratified into A and B. Product group A could be supplied either from stock to the distributor in 2 to 5 days including transit time, or had to be produced from the numerous inventory points in 21 days but to this was added the 42 days it took to plan the work. The 42 days to plan was an incredible waste and could be eliminated as shown in Stage 1.

The results would be spectacular as shown in Table 10.1. A supermarket holding point for an intermediate stage of production was set up and the production time to satisfy orders was reduced to one-to-five days and the delivery to the distributor reduced to 10 to 17 days by simply applying the 26 Rules for Lean Systems. Stage 3 could reduce it further to 4 to 11 days into the distributor's store.

Table 10.1 Staged planning cycle changes for A and B showing increased velocity (days)

Group	A			B		
	Before	Stage 1	Stage 2	Stage 3	Stage 4	Stage 5
Planning	42	7	1	42	7	1
Production	21	1 to 5	1 to 5	70	14	7 to 14
Shipment	2 to 5	2 to 5	2 to 5	2 to 5	2 to 5	2 to 5
	65 to 68	10 to 17	4 to 11	114 to 117	23 to 26	10 to 20

Product Group B was a lot more complicated, but the 26 Rules for Lean Systems still applied and as shown in Table 10.1, the 114 to 117 days could be reduced to 10 to 20 days with the correct parameters in place. This was only the beginning of the improvement. The next stage was to increase the value-added percent by optimising batch sizes and minimising setups using SMED and the 22 Creative Ideas for Innovation and the SMED Rule 25 and Rule 19 mainly.

When all the above was implemented to Stage 2 the working capital was reduced by $40 million, sales of the fast-moving lines increased as in the past sales were suffering because of poor inventory control, and lack of stock, the on-time deliveries improved from 32.6% to 95% and then 99% inside 2.7 years. The company went from a loss to a profit of $40 million (EBITA) on sales of approximately $300 million.

There are other improvements that can be made. Here, for this client, the planning cycles are synchronised between a major supplier and the customer. In this case, when the plan was implemented the raw material inventory at the customer was reduced from $1.5 million to $100,000 and the supplier reduced his price by 5%, the holding cost at his plant was reduced enormously.

The Rules for Lean Systems, when used in a common sense fashion, will always lead to significant improvements in productivity and profit. By speeding up the planning system and using the correct input data, the velocity had increased.

World trade is largely dependent on adding value to goods. The closer the company is to the end user, the better the enterprise is able to control product and process flow and profit. Japan has shown us that new standards can be set by applying statistical tools to reduce variation, i.e. Statistical Process Control (SPC). Before we can take advantage of SPC, we must get the setup right and remove the special causes affecting the process. Lean aimed at cycle-time reduction and increased velocity uses team problem-solving, the scientific method and practices process intent. There are significant stages in introducing lean statistically to the shop-floor after the planning system is fixed, as follows:

Stage 1: Acceptance sampling

Use accept/reject systems to quickly determine the special causes of variation.

Stage 2: Statistical Process Control (SPC)

Use prevention and run charts to further improve the process and aim to reduce variation and introduce the concept of process capability. This can produce the 3 ppm Six Sigma control but in some cases it may be necessary for large sophisticated processes and machinery to go to experimental design.

Stage 3: Experimental design

Isolate the major variables and reduce variation using Taguchi statistical techniques.

SMEs in Australia – particularly in the Service Industry, which lags Manufacturing – are mainly in Stage 1. We need to progress to Stage 2 urgently – Australia must increase its productivity. Australia must continue to add value to its raw materials. If our goods are to complete in the global marketplace, we must add value to products in areas where we have a natural SAW in areas of import replacement. Once again, we must achieve export success by increasing productivity and improving quality.

When the manufacturing time, M, is greater than the expected delivery time demanded by the customer, D, then the enterprise has no choice but to Make to Stock (MTS). This is, of course, the most expensive option, since holding inventory increases working capital, interest expenses, redundancies waste and write-downs and encourages over-production.

Many companies now practice the Dell model. Dell assemble from order and so hold components in stock and start assembling after the order is placed and the money received. This is good for the cashflow of Dell, but not the customer.

ZARA International, led by the owner Amancio Ortega, use high-velocity supply chains from cheap labour areas all over the world to make fashion garments and 'push' new fashion to buyers with no redundancies in the store, since they always slightly undersupply. Their raw materials are sourced anywhere and shipped direct to the converter.

Toyota are trialling Make to Order cars in Japan and like Honda and Mercedes are introducing an agency model instead of a dealer model to cut costs toe the customer and remove variation in price between dealers. The cars ae to be sold at a fixed price with no variation or price reductions. The price is set by the manufacturer.

Make To Order books by Canon are a reality. In fact, an earlier book of mine is an example of the 26 Rules for Lean Systems for improving productivity to supply the printed book market.

As well, this book was sold with a batch size of one. The maximum stock level will therefore be zero. The turnaround time for a batch is one day from order placed to production of a copy. The delivery time to the customer is therefore currently one day plus transit time to the customer. The customer can also place an order, pay into my account and then either receive a hardcopy or download a digital copy for a cheaper price.

Whilst it has been clear for some time that the virtual digital processes will turn conventional businesses upside down the speed with which the opportunities have been seized by industry has been reasonably fast for big business but very slow for the small to medium sized enterprises.

Even in the car retailing industry the speed of application and implementation of the new digital virtual business models has only just begun with the introduction of the agency model for sale.

More and more people will work from home and the long costly commute to work in big cities will almost disappear. The cost here however is a cultural one as the nature of human interaction changes.

This is our digital future. It is about lean velocity, people cooperating, process aimed at precision and high-quality, and perfect processes at Six Sigma, people, process and precision ... the essence of velocity using lean systems and Six Sigma. This can be achieved with a lean business framework and the correct application of the appropriate tools in industry 4.0. Halving production lead time doubles throughput and reduces cost by over 20% and reduces inventory by up to 50%.

Globalisation and the speed of the digital economy are accelerating the rate of change of business as never before. Trade and commercial barriers are being shattered by the explosion in information technology as the nation states of the world open up to form a global village. The resulting evolution in data interchange and knowledge has increased the speed of the supply chains to the customer and the flow of capital between the chain's links. However, it has also increased the complexity of hew decision making processes and magnified the risk of errors.

To combat this business leadership by boards and executives must be more creative and highly skilled. Brain power will prevail.

Successful businesses of the future will quickly separate themselves from the rest as they accept the challenge of being more innovative.

Successful companies will be:

- Led by a CEO and Board with a good strategic understanding and good numeracy skills and a good team of advisers who will collect the necessary data precisely and immediately.
- Using the latest information and intelligence-based technology. Information that has to be available to a learning focussed workforce.
- Mobile and flexible operational teams and management groups continuously monitoring their effectiveness and shifts in the marketplace. This must be process focussed not functionally focussed.
- Using teams operated by front line staff with significant autonomy to improve service to the customer.
- Structured in a tightly controlled manner and hence will be able to move quickly and be able to take advantage of cultural and perceptive swings in the marketplace.
- Focused on a reduced time to market for new products that will quickly sort out the leaders from the followers.
- Able to recognise that there is a strong link between product development and process development and innovation.
- Lean at high velocity of the whole of the supply chain and in all internal functional groups is the way. It is the CEO's responsibility to lead the restructuring and implementation of these new ideas and work practices and technology. The CEO must lead and innovate at an accelerated rate or his company will disappear in its competitive environment.

As can be seen from this discussion, the key elements are a good Vision and strategic plan, a good lean business structure and the correct application of the appropriate industry 4.0 tools.

Modern technology will enable business to respond to key challenges more quickly. The problems however will not be purely technical but will be cultural and new disciplines will need to be learned by all. This means and increasing amount of technical and cultural change at a read rate. The future is about velocity.

Appendix: Definitions

A, B, C Classification	An arbitrary grouping of Stock Keeping Units (SKU's) enabling different rules for production and inventory control. As a first pass, the groupings are: • A = Products with a high volume of sales and a low risk of being unsold if kept as stock. Hence, they are MTS (Made-To-Stock). • B = Products that have a smaller volume than A but are to be manufactured with finished goods stock but with lower inventory levels. • C = Products with a high risk that will not be held in stock but instead are MTO (Made-To-Order).
AGVS	Automated Guided Vehicle System
AMH	Automated Materials Handling
AMT	Advanced Manufacturing Technology
Analytical Tools	1. Brainstorming 2. Imagineering 3. Flowchart – Value Stream Maps 4. Data Collection 5. Check Sheets 6. Run Charts 7. Histograms 8. Magic Lanterns 9. Statistics 10. Dispersion 11. Cause and Effect Diagrams 12. Pareto Chart 13. Team Problem Solving 14. Control Charts 15. Method Sheets and Setup Sheets 16. Computers 17. Memory (History) 18. Training and Education 19. Communication 20. Shewhart Wheels (SDCA, PDCA)

Artificial Intelligence	Attribution of human skills to inanimate objects
Asset Turnover	A measure of the efficiency of the company defined as Sales divided by Total Assets.
ATC	Automated Tool Changeover
Attribute Data	Go/No Go or Yes/No or count data
Autonomation	A word coined to describe a feature of the Toyota production system whereby a machine is designed to stop automatically whenever a defective is produced.
Average Collection Period	A measure of the efficiency of the company defined as Accounts Receivable divided by Sales per Day.
Balanced Scorecard	A series of measurements in all business functions
Bayes Rule	Machine Learning...Python
Bell Curve	The Normal Distribution; the shape of the probability density distribution when a large number of random variables affect a measurable variable. The shape is perfectly symmetrical and bell shaped.
Benchmarking	Is an ongoing, systematic process to search for and introduce international best practice into your own organization, conducted in such a way that all parts of your organization understand and achieve their full potential.
Blockchain	Encrypted interlocked records
Brainstorming	Synergistic idea development in a team environment
Business Process Re-Engineering	Order-of magnitude improvement in key business processes – by radical changes in these processes (often using information technology).
CAD/CAM	Computer Aided Design/Computer Aided Manufacture
CAD	Computer Aided Design and Drafting
CAE	Computer Aided Engineering
CAIT	Computer Aided Inspection and Testing
Capability	Measurement of spread of variation when the system or process is stable compared with specification limits.

Capacity	The ability of manufacturing to meet market demand
Capacity Amount	The size of capacity increment added
Capacity Timing	The time at which capacity increases are 'triggered' – ahead of, in step with or behind demand.
Capital Expenditure	The use of today's funds to generate tomorrows profits
Capital Structure	The proportional relationship between debt and equity
CAPM	Computer Aided Production Management
CAPP	Computer Aided Process Planning
Cause and Effect Diagram	An analytical technique used to analyse and organize a problem or process when there are many causes of variation – called also Ishikawa, Fishbone or Dead Ned Diagram.
Changeover Time	The time between finishing a batch runs on a piece of equipment and starting the next (dissimilar) batch.
Check Points and Control Points	Both check points and control points are used in measuring the progress of improvement related activities between differing managerial levels. Check points represent process-oriented criteria. Control points represent result-oriented criteria.
Check Sheet	A simple tool used for collecting or gathering attribute data and presenting the data in an organized, logical and readily understood manner.
CIM	Computer Integrated Manufacturing
CNC	Computer Numerical Control
Cloud Computing	Connection to a wide range of digital tools via the internet
Commitment	The employees' motivation, understanding and response to management's communications about changes in the environment – only achieved with the right level of mutual trust.
Common causes of Variation	Chance causes of variation, which are traceable directly to the system. They are purely random.
Communication	Any action or behaviour, which results in an exchange of meaning.
Competence	The level of employee versatility, skills and perspective to take on new roles and jobs.

Competitive Advantage	A measure of the organisational advantage over competitors.
Competitive Arena	The overall influence that other suppliers have on customers.
Congruence (of goals)	The degree of compatibility between the goals of the individual and the goals of the company.
Consignment	Inventory, usually raw material is held at the customers' premises and paid for on agreed terms as it is used. The customer only pays on usage while the vendor, the supplier, wears the capital cost of the inventory held on consignment. In addition, the customer pays for the storage costs in terms of the building capital, rent and racks. This is very similar to VMI (Vendor Managed Inventory).
Constraint	Bottleneck, Pacesetter for a system process that determines the overall throughput or production of the whole system.
Control	To regulate or restrain, constrain
Control Chart	A tool used for graphically indicating whether a process is stable and performing at the correct level. It consists of a run chart with variation limits (UCL, LCL) displayed. Specification units are often also displayed.
CONWIP	Continuous Work In Progress; an acronym to describe the concept that the work in progress does not ever reside in inventory and inventory is regarded as a waste not an asset.
Core Competencies	Are fundamental building blocks on which any enterprise bases its ability to satisfy and exceed the expectations of its customers? They provide the basis for the development of core products and their variants (end products): the concept applies to both the goods and services components.
Cost Effectiveness	The organisations relative human resources costs as measured by such direct factors as wages, benefits and indirect costs such as strikes, staff turnover and other grievances (people context).

Cost of Quality	The difference between the actual cost to a company of making and selling products and the cost which would exist if there were no failures and no possibility of failure of the product, in conforming to specifications during manufacture and use.
Coverage Ratio	A measure of the debt capacity of the company and its level of financial risk, and defined as Profits before Interest and Tax divided by Interest.
22 Creative Ideas	1. Properties 2. Space 3. Order 4. Energy 5. Shape 6. Movement 7. Friction 8. Magnetism (attraction, affinity) 9. Gravity 10. Dissecting 11. Fragmenting 12. Self-service 13. Copying 14. Coatings 15. Blending 16. Phases 17. Solvent 18. Oxidation 19. Potential 20. Combination 21. Multi-use 22. Prevention
Critical Success Factors	Those things that must be done well to ensure the future success of the business.
Cross-Functional Management	The interdepartmental coordination required realizing the policy goals of a KAIZEN and a Total Quality Control program. After corporate strategy and planning are determined, top management sets objectives for cross-functional efforts that cut laterally throughout the organisation.

Culture	Is learned behaviour and knowledge that is integrated by a group, shared among group members and passed along to descendants.
Current Ratio	A measure of the liquidity of the company defined as Current Assets divided by Current Liabilities.
Customer	A person who buys goods or services from a business, a person one has to deal with. In any business there are internal and external customers.
Customer Expectations	A combination of customer needs and preferences for opportunities to be realised, problems to be solved and good feelings to be created.
Customer Needs	Those essential requirements of customers which must be satisfied by the goods and services response
Customer Preferences	Those non-essential requirements which customers desire to be satisfied by the goods and services response.
DBMS	Database Management System
DBR	Drum, Butter, Rope (visual manufacturing)
Debt Ratio	A measure of the debt capacity of the company and its level of financial risk and defined as Total Liabilities divided by Total Assets.
Debt/Equity Ratio	A measure of the debt capacity of the company and its level of financial risk and defined as Total Liabilities divided by Shareholders' Equity.
Deming	Dr Deming was the statistician who was sent to Japan by General Douglas Macarthur after the second World War to introduce a new quality-based manufacturing philosophy. This led to techniques such as TQC (Total Quality Control), TQM (Total Quality Management), and SPC (Statistical Process Control). Dr. Deming developed a 14-point plan for management.
Deming's 14 Points	1. Create and publish to all employees a statement of the aims and purposes of the company or other organization. The management must demonstrate constantly their commitment to this statement. 2. Learn the new philosophy, top management and everybody.

	3. Understand the purpose of inspection, for improvement of process and reduction on cost. 4. End the practice of awarding business on the basis of price tag alone. 5. Improve constantly and forever the system of production and service. 6. Institute training for skills. 7. Teach and Institute leadership. 8. Drive out fear. Create trust. Create a climate of innovation. 9. Optimise toward the aims and purposes of the company the efforts of teams, groups, staff areas too. 10. Eliminate exhortations for the workforce. 11. (a) Eliminate numerical quotas for production. Instead, learn and institute methods for improvement. (b) Eliminate Management by Objectives (MBO). Instead, learn the capabilities of the processes and how to improve them. 12. Remove barriers that rob people of pride of work. 13. Encourage education and self-improvement for everyone. 14. Take action to accomplish the transformation.
Desired Outcome	Statement driven by the sustainable competitive advantage to guide decision making.
Differentiation	The uniqueness of the business with respect to its competitors as perceived by the market.
Discounted Cash Flow	Technique used in evaluating multi-year capital investments. There are two popular variants: internal rate of return and net present value.
Dividend Yield	A measure of market value defined as Dividends per Share divided by Market Price per Share.
DNC	Direct Numerical Control
Earnings per share (EPS)	A measure of market value defined as Net Income divided by the number of Common shares on issue.

EBET	Equal Batches Every Time; as far as possible the batch size or run length for intermediate processes should be fixed so that one run can be readily compared with another. For the ultimate system BTO (Built-To-Order), the run length will be highly variable and will match the customers' orders, but this will only be possible with rapid setups and where the setup cost effect on the direct manufacturing cost is small.
EDI	Electronic Data Interchange
Efficiency	The ratio of actual to standard performance – most often (unfortunately) associated with the measurement of direct labour performance.
Emotion	Intense mental feeling, love, hate.
Employee Influence	How employees can act to improve or protect their economic share, psychological satisfaction and rights.
Employee Involvement	The involvement of employees in the creative process of continuously improving the company's ability to support the sustainable competitive advantage.
Enterprise Development Plan	A summary of the key actions that the client is undertaking and intends to undertake, to develop and improve their business (produced by the company in conjunction with its AusIndustry Case Officer).
Enterprise Vision	Refer to 'Vision' definition
Environment	The overall influence governments, regulations and public opinion have on customers and suppliers.
EPR	Economic Production Run; the optimum batch size for production. This is heavily influenced by the setup and the inventory level, ideally with a Kanban system. For a simple inventory control and purchase order system, the equivalent term used is usually called the EOQ (Economic Order Quantity).
ERP	Enterprise Resource Planning; an extension of the MRP system to include extra processes and systems.
Facility	Size, location and focus of plant(s)

FIFO	First In First Out; a rule for inventory control to avoid stock damage and loss and old stock being sold after new stock.
Financial Limit to Growth	An approximate calculation to assess the maximum sustainable annual growth rate in the short-term.
Financial Strategy	The pattern of decisions required maximising the profits generated by the company's overall investment in pursuing sustainable competitive advantage.
Five S Process (with Six S Process)	These are visual tools to improve productivity. They are based on the Five Pillars of the visual workplace (Hirooyuki Hirano): 1. Sort 2. Set in Order 3. Shine 4. Standardise 5. Sustain 6. Safety
Flowchart	A pictorial summary of the flow of various steps of a process.
FG	Finished Goods
FMC	Flexible Manufacturing Cell
FMS	Flexible Manufacturing System
Focus	The degree of scope in the business, often defined in product or market terms.
Frequency Table	A simple tool used to show in tabular form the frequency or number of times a given value occurs in a set of data.
Functional Layout	A batch production process layout with equipment grouped according to machine function.
Funnel Experiment	A demonstration of how tampering with a process will increase the variability. In this experiment, a funnel is set up above a target and marbles are dropped into it. The design is such that the marbles are very much smaller in diameter than the inside diameter of the neck of the funnel. The result is that the marbles spray into a distribution around the target. Since the first drop will most probably miss,

	then the operator will invariably adjust the funnel thinking it will improve the likelihood that the next marble will hit the target bullseye. With 26 drops with and without moving the funnel, it is clearly demonstrated that moving the funnel between drops increases the distribution or spread of the scores; that is, tampering makes the system worse.
Globalization	The term used to describe the change in trading and interaction dynamics resulting from the reduction in trade barriers, the formation of trade blocs, increased global competition due to accelerated supply chains and increased ease of market access, and the result of real time IT data and its analysis.
Governing Values	Refer to 'Values' definitions
Gross Margin (GM)	The difference between the selling price (S) and cost of raw materials including freight (COS). Hence, GM is equal to Gross Profit (GP). This is not a scientific measurement and its use and definition vary from one industry to another. In many cases direct manufacturing costs and labour and other costs are included.
GT	Group Technology
Histogram	A graphical technique used to illustrate the distribution of a set of data values. It is the frequency of an event plotted against the magnitude of the event.
Human Dynamics	The process of interaction between people, one-on-one or in groups.
Human Resources Flow	The flow of people into, through and out of the organisation
Human Resources Strategy	The pattern of decisions influencing the relationship between organisation and employees in jointly pursuing sustainable competitive advantage.
Imagineering	A process of brainstorming involving comparing the real system with the ideal system and comparing the differences and then prioritizing these so that a course of action can be defined.

Improvement	Improvement as a part of a successful KAIZEN strategy goes beyond the dictionary definition of the word. Improvement is a mind-set inextricably linked to maintaining and improving standards. In a still broader sense, improvement can be defined as KAIZEN and innovation, where a KAIZEN strategy maintains and improves the working standard, gradual improvements and innovation calls forth radical improvements as a result of large investments in technology and equipment.
Incoming Material Control	Involves the receiving and stocking of those parts whose quality conforms to the specification requirements, with emphasis upon the fullest practical supplier responsibility.
Information Input	The process of understanding, interpreting and defining customers' goods and services needs and preferences.
Innovation	1. Taking opportunities to enhance products and processes by systematic, timely and achievable advances. 2. Application of new ideas to products and processes or organizations resulting in significant benefits in quality, cost, delivery and features.
Innovation Strategy	The pattern of decisions directed to product and process 'innovation' in pursuing the sustainable competitive advantage.
Input	The process of understanding, interpreting and defining customers' goods and services, needs and preferences.
Interpersonal Activities	Involves interaction between people to produce intangible outcomes; the outcomes are usually assessed in evaluative terms.
Inventory Turnover	A measure of the efficiency of the company defined as Cost of Goods Sold divided by Finished Goods Inventory
JIT	Just In Time
KAIZEN	KAIZEN means improvement. Moreover, it means continuing improvement in personal life, home life, social life and working life. When applied to the

	workplace, KAIZEN means continuing improvement involving everyone – managers and workers alike.
Kanban	A communication tool in the 'Just-In-Time' production and inventory control system. Usually a card at shop floor level but can be an electronic packet.
Key Principles	Of the customer supplier relationship • 'All people serve customers through a system' • All systems are contaminated with variation' • 'Variation dominates the ability of people in the system to satisfy customers'
KPD	Key Performance Drivers, KPM for the input side of the process. These are not easily measured for the service industry but if quantified, useful information can be obtained.
KPI	Key Process Indicators; these are real time measurements in the same sense that Jazz is real time composition. If they deviate from control, then action can be taken immediately to prevent the KPO measurements being outside the desired control range. This is called preventive action.
KPM	Key Performance Measures; these may be KPD, KPI, KPO.
KPO	Key Performance Outputs. These are the after the event. Measurements that are very important, but require corrective action if they indicate a problem.
Law of Finance	For every operating action there is a financial reaction
Lean Manufacturing	Lean Manufacturing may be defined as the production of goods with minimum working capital, minimum inventory, maximum speed, minimum waste, on time, of the correct quality, to the customer's specification. This is done using systems that aim at continuous flow and maximum flexibility using a pull system instead of a push system. Lean Manufacturing is about efficiently manufacturing a large range of products on short runs. It emphasises quality, value added and process control.

Lean Thinking 26 Rules	• **People**
	1. Continuously improve the culture
	2. Team-up
	3. Optimise customer response
	• **Integration**
	4. Supply equals demand
	5. 'Pull' for minimum cycle-time
	6. Apply to supply chain
	7. Minimise variation
	8. Shorten the financial cycle
	9. Apply *6S System*
	• **Planning**
	10. Demand to bottleneck
	11. Even mix for production
	12. First in first and prioritise
	13. Optimize supply
	14. Load-levelling
	15. Equal batches at the Economic Production Run (EPR)
	16. Optimise sequencing
	• **Operations**
	17. Minimize waste
	18. Aim for continuous flow
	19. Maximise value-added
	20. Link processes
	21. Match processes
	22. Minimise hold points
	23. Prevention not rework
	24. Use Statistical Process Control (SPC) to improve control to Six Sigma
	25. Use Single Minute Exchange of Dies (SMED)
	26. Use quality systems as part of the business processes
Lead Time (manufacturing)	The actual elapsed time those materials are present in the production process. Unfortunately, the definition is not precise. For the more general case, it is the time between order placed and delivery.

Leadership	Attention through vision, meaning through communication, trust through positioning, positive self-regard. Ability to generate followers through action, trust, integrity, deeds, commitment, communication or charisma.
Learning Organization	One skilled at creating acquiring and transferring knowledge, and at modifying its behavior to reflect new knowledge and insights. Term developed by Royal Dutch Shell and popularized by Senge (1990).
Low Cost Position	The lowest cost producer with respect to competitors
Magic Lanterns	Visual graphic illustrations of data and information
Maintenance	Refers to activities that are directed to maintaining current technological, managerial and operating standards.
Manufacture	The making of goods or wares by labour or machinery
Manufacturing	A competitive weapon rather than a set of ponderous resources and constraints.
Manufacturing Function	The structure and infrastructure of design, production and suppliers, including associated information, systems, technology and materials.
Manufacturing Process Technology	The total system of equipment, people and procedures used to design and produce the firm's products and services.
Manufacturing Strategy	The pattern of decisions directed to creating continuous improvement in manufacturing capability in order to create and sustain the competitive advantage.
Mark up (MU)	Mark up is usually expressed the extra amount in dollars which is added to the cost of the raw materials to yield the selling price (retail price usually).
Market	Set of all actual and potential buyers of a product
Market Segmentation	Division of the market into separate product/customer groups each of which contains customers with (relatively) uniform expectations.
Marketing	Getting the right products and services to the right people at the right place at the right price with the right communication and promotion.

Marketing Mix	Positioning the products to meet customer needs and to sustain the competitive advantage by means of the 4 P's: Product, Price, Place, Promotion.
Marketing Strategy	The pattern of decisions required developing the growth links between the business and its customers in pursuing sustainable competitive advantage.
Markup	The extra amount ($) which is added to the cost of the raw materials to yield the selling price.
Mission	Concise, single statement of future business content, direction and scope.
Moments of Truth	Any episode in which the customer forms an opinion regarding the ability of the supplier's response in goods and services to meet expectations.
MRP	Material Requirements Planning
MRP-II	Manufacturing Resources Planning
MTO	Made-To-Order
MTS	Made-To-Stock
NC	Numerical Control
Normal Distribution	A 'bell-shaped' natural distribution of process outcomes described by the average (mean) and spread (standard deviation) of the resultant outcomes.
Operational Activities	Involves definable processes producing tangible outcomes; the outcomes are usually assessed in quantifiable terms.
Organic Improvement	The internally generated improvement in total effectiveness as measured by trends in performance parameters over time.
Organization of Work	Particular combination of job task, technology, skills, management style and personnel policies and practices; that is, the definition and design of work. The choices lie in the generic areas of 'bureaucratic' (employee involved as subordinate), 'market' (employee involved as contractor) or 'clan' (employee involved as member).

Organizational Effectiveness (Strategy)	A measure of the organisation's ability to achieve goals. Having decided where we wish to position the company in the marketplace, the enterprise must improve its organizational effectiveness. This means it must improve its process and system capability. Here, the system capability is mathematically equal to the product of the process efficiencies.
Outcome	The result of activity, e.g. product, service. This may be tangible or intangible, subjective, or objective.
P & IPC	Production and Inventory Planning and Control
Pacesetter	The Pacesetter process is the process that is the major constraint on the system. The idea is to send a demand signal to the pacesetter and pull through from there.
Pareto Chart	An analytical technique which identifies and ranks the major problems to be solved in order of significance, e.g. the 80/20 rule after Vilfredo Pareto. 20% of the causes give rise to 80% of the effect or 80% of your sales comes from 20% of your customers.
PDCA Cycle (Plan-Do-Check-Act)	The PDCA Cycle – Plan, Do, Check, Act – is an adaptation of the Shewhart Wheel. Where the Shewhart Wheel stresses the need for constant interaction among research, design, production and sales, the PDCA Cycle asserts that every managerial action can be improved by careful application of the sequence: Plan, Do, Check, Act.
Perception Points	Any episode in which the customer forms an opinion regarding the ability of the supplier's response to meet expectations.
Place Issues	Channels, coverage locations, inventory and transport
Plant Life Cycle	The aging stages a plant facility moves through – these being initial planning and start up, incremental expansion, maturation and reinvestment and renewal or shut down.
Poka Yoke	'Mistake proofing' a system

Policy (Japan)	In Japan the term is used to describe long and medium-range management orientations as well as annual goals or targets. Another aspect of policy is that it is composed of both goals and measures; that is, both ends and means. Goals are usually quantitative figures established by top management, such as sales, profit and market share targets. Measures, on the other hand are the specific action programs to achieve these goals. A goal that is not expressed in terms of such specific measures is merely a slogan. It is imperative that top management determines both the goals and the measures and then 'deploys' them down through the organisation.
Policy Deployment	The process of implementing the policies of a KAIZEN program directly through line managers and indirectly through cross-functional organisation.
Policy Prioritization	A technique to ensure maximum utilization of resources at all levels of management in the process of policy deployment. Top management's policy statement must be restated at all management levels in increasingly specific and action-oriented goals, eventually becoming precise, quantitative values.
Positioning (strategy)	Positioning equals strategic positioning. One of the two major elements of strategic planning. It is a description of where in the overall market the company places its products and services with respect to the market, particularly with reference to market share and market growth. Other characteristics will also be included at a later stage of the analysis. Companies strategically position themselves to gain a strategic advantage, or create a strategic advantage or to take advantage of newly created marketplace opportunities or technological advantages. The other major element of strategic planning is "organisational effectiveness".
Preventive Action	Also called Preventative action. Action taken to prevent the need for corrective action or rework. Also designing possible human errors out of the system.

Price Issues	List price, discounts, allowances, payment periods and credit terms.
Price/Earnings Ratio	A measure of market value defined as Market Price per Share divided by Earnings per Share.
Procedure	Details of purpose and scope of the process which identify how, when, why and by whom the activity is to be performed.
Procedures Manual	A specific document, detailing the purpose and scope of the nominated process, which identifies who does what, when, where, how and why. The Procedures Manual normally is a companion set of documents to the Quality Manual in a QA accreditation project and is often called a Quality System Procedures Manual.
Process	The method by which the input is converted or combined to create the output or simply the conversion of an input to an output via a series of activities. The six parts to a process are: 1. Setup (preparation) 2. Run (the value added part) 3. Maintenance (preventive to avoid breakdowns) 4. Breakdown (errors and Rework) 5. Idle (available to run, but not utilised) 6. Cleanup
Process Configuration	The way the manufacturing process is organized and operated – project, job, batch, assembly or continuous.
Process factors	The interacting features of the method, which affect the output.
Process Improvement	Involves investigation and tests to locate the cause of non-conforming parts and excessive part-to-part variation, to determine the solution required and ensure that improvement and corrective action are permanent and complete.
Process Innovation	Identifying improved methods of adding value to the product.
Process Input	Materials and services entering the process, which are converted or combined to create the output.

Process Intent	The required operating characteristics and outputs for the process.
Process Output	The materials and services leaving the process, which are the result of the input being converted or combined by the process.
Process Parameters	The interacting features of the method, which can be changed to affect the output.
Process-Oriented Management	A style of management that is also people oriented in contrast to one that is oriented solely toward results. In process-oriented management a manager must support and stimulate efforts to improve the way employees do their jobs. Such a style of management calls for a long-term outlook and usually requires some behavioral change.
Product	Something produced (service, outcome, ware, goods)
Product based Layout	A batch production process layout with equipment grouped according to product group.
Product Control	Involves the control or production and field service so that departures from quality specifications can be corrected before defective or non-conforming products are produced and the proper service can be maintained in the field to assure full provision of the intended customer satisfaction.
Product Flow	The flow of materials and parts into, through and out of the production process.
Product Innovation	That extra 'something' that differentiates a product from its predecessors in satisfying a customer need, be it an enhancement of an old product or a new product development.
Product Issues	Quality features, options, style, brand name, packaging, sizes, services, warranties and returns.
Product Life Cycle	That period of time for which a product is acceptable to the market – normally the cycle consists of development, growth, maturity and decline stages.
Product Portfolio Analysis	An analytical approach designed to identify product performers and non-performers, to set product priorities for allocations of cash in order to reposition products and to establish a target portfolio, balanced with respect to cash.

Product Proliferation	The growth of product range over time
Product/Need Congruence	The degree of 'fit' between the market or customer need and the actual product response.
Product/Process Match	Relationship between product life cycle and process life cycle
Production Planning/ Material Control and Information Systems	Planned flow, coordination and control of materials information and associated resources into, within and out of production.
Products	All deliverables to a customer, including service – sum of all responses.
Profit Margin (Return on Sales [ROI])	A measure of the profit making efficiency of the firm, and equal to Net Income divided by Total Sales.
Project ROI	The particular annual interest rate which would cause the present value of the projected net cash flow to be zero for the investment in question.
Promotion Issues	Advertising, personal, selling, sales, promotion and publicity.
Pull	The Pull system relies on satisfying demand with a short lead-time by pulling the product through the system when the demand is there, not making to stock and taking the risk and the extra cost. Kanban cards can be used.
Push	The old system of making to stock or inventory and hoping the demand is there or going out and prospecting.
QC (Quality Control)	A system of means to economically produce goods or services that satisfy customer requirements.
QC Circles	Quality Control Circles
Quality	Always means uniformity. Dependability, reliability at low cost suited to the market – within specification and with minimum variation. This applies to product and process.
Quality Assurance	All those planned and systematic actions necessary to provide adequate confidence that goods or services will satisfy given expectations.

Quality Assurance Accreditation Project	To develop and implement a prescribed Quality Assurance system as the basis for sustained continuous improvement. The purpose of accreditation is to undertake an audit of the prescribed QA system by an external party to establish its conformance to a standard or agreed level.
Quality Audit	A planned and documented activity performed in accordance with written procedures and checklists to verify by investigation and the examination and evaluation of objective evidence, that applicable elements of a quality program or plan have been developed documented and effectively implemented with a specified requirement.
Quality Control	Total composite product and service characteristics of marketing, manufacture and maintenance through which the product and service is use will meet or exceed the customer expectations.
Quality Manual	A concise document setting out the general quality policies, procedures and practices of an organisation
Quality Mission	Statement outlining the key quality characteristics of the company in the future – includes vision. Includes the key policy statement of the company and a statement of future business direction and scope.
Quality Perceptions	The opinion of customers regarding the ability of the supplier's response to meet their needs and preferences.
Quick Response	A system of supply focusing on a reduction of lead-time from supplier to end customer. This leads to a reduction in waste, working capital, inventory.
Quality System	A four-tiered system linking: • Quality Policy • Quality Systems Procedures • Work Instructions • Quality Records
Quick Ratio	A measure of the liquidity of the company defined as Current Assets less Inventory divided by current Liabilities.
QWL	Quality of Working Life

R (Range) Chart	A graphical technique used to measure dispersion or spread of the process. Can detect changes in the stability of process.
Response	The output from the supplier's value adding system to meet the customer's goods and services needs and preferences.
Results Oriented Management	This style of management is well established in the West and emphasises controls, performance, results, rewards (usually financial), or the denial of rewards and even penalties. Criteria or R Criteria are easily quantifiable and short term. Western style management emphasizes R Criteria almost exclusively.
Retail	The sales of goods in small quantities directly to a customer – to sell in small quantities by the piece
Return on Assets	A measure of the profit making efficiency of the company and equal to the net income divided by the total company assets.
Return on Equity	A measure of the profitability of the firm, and equal to Net Income divided by Shareholders' Equity.
Return on Investment (ROI)	A measure of the profit making efficiency of the firm, and equal to Net Income divided by Total Assets.
Reward Systems	Tangible and 'personal' systems by which organisations reward competent employees in return for performance and loyalty.
RF	Radio Frequency. A communication technique employing handheld devices to communicate from the Point Of Sale (POS) or Point Of Demand (POD) to a central server.
RPO	Reverse Purchase Order; after goods are sold at a retail outlet, an automatic order is electronically generated on the supplier for replacement.
Run Chart	Plot variable or attribute versus time or consecutive number
Scattergram	An analytical technique used to determine whether any relationship exists between two given variables and whether one variable is a function of (or controlled by) another variable.

SDCA (Standardise-Do-Check-Act)	A refinement of the PDCA Cycle wherein management decides first to establish the standard before performing the regular PDCA function.
Service	This is a product or outcome delivered to serve or satisfy a need of a customer. Good service is the delivery of a satisfactory outcome which meets or exceeds a customer's needs.
Service Industry	An organisation linking producers and consumers
Seven Tools (original)	1. Check Sheet 2. Run Chart 3. Histogram 4. Scattergram 5. Pareto Diagram 6. Cause and Effect Diagram 7. Control chart
SFC	Shop Floor Control
Shewhart Wheels	PDCA or SDCA, see earlier
Sigma (σ)	Sigma is a standard deviation
Six Sigma (6σ)	A measure of the spread or dispersion of a series of measurements for a normal distribution. 99.7% of all measurements for normal distribution fall between $\pm$ 3σ, hence 6σ covers 99.7% of all measurements. However, a 6σ company as defined by Motorola is closer to a $\pm$ 6σ = 12σ. Motorola however allow for a 1.5 sigma shift of the average. Honda in the Saitama plant in Tokyo possibly work at 7 sigma. Our hospitals are probably at 2 sigma.
Seven Sigma (7σ)	Target plus or minus 7 Standard deviations without the 1.5 sigma target shift allowed for with six sigma, all within the tolerance level for the process.
SMED	Single Minute Exchange of Dies. The principle here is to continuously reduce setups until dies are exchanged in a minute and the setup lost time is reduced to a goal of zero by carrying out the setup concurrently off line.

SPC	Statistical Process Control; a method of using statistical data to improve the predictability of the outcomes from processes. It involves process measurement, frequency analysis and the elimination of special causes of variation and the systematic reduction in the spread of the variation due to common causes and then the introduction of control charts and capability indices (after Shewhart and Deming).
Stable Process	A process that is in statistical control, free of special causes and has an outcome that is random (yet predicted) within defined variation limits (called Control Limited).
Standardised Work	As defined at Toyota this is the optimum combination of workers, machines and materials.
Standards	A set of policies, rules, directives and procedures established by management for all major operations, which serves as guidelines that enable all employees to perform their jobs successfully.
Statistics	The study of numerical data to better understand the characteristics of a population or process.
Strategic Advantage for Winning (SAW)	Those special capabilities identified by the company that will enable it to attain a sustainable position in the market with respect to major competitors. It is like an SCA (Sustainable Competitive Advantage), but recognizes that no competitive advantage remains an advantage for long in the global market. The SAW overlays the competitive advantages of all segments, groups' products, and services.
Strategic Factors	Those strategically oriented aspects of the company which have a major influence on the achievement of the company-wide goal of continuous improvement. Factors include goods and services competitiveness, operational reliability and human resources effectiveness.
Strategy	A consistent pattern of decisions actually made to gain a sustainable competitive advantage.

Strategy Map	A plot (graph of 2 variables [x & y]) designed to present a graphical illustration of the current position of your business (ONE), and illustrating the future opportunities that can be created when both the internal and external strategic issues are taken into account. In this model, 7 strategy maps are used. The idea is to encourage a statistical approach.
Structure of Production	The linkages and relationships between discrete manufacturing operations and associated structure and infrastructure elements.
Subjective	Existing in a person's mind and not existing outside it.
Sub-Unit Focus	The production process layout according to either process function grouping or product grouping
Supermarket	An array of products or components arranged in a convenient fashion to enable visual control and easy access to feed a process.
Supply Chain	The sum of the links between companies describing the flow of goods and services from raw material to end user. For example, in the conversion of bauxite to aerospace parts the supply chain consists of Mine bauxite at Weipa > convert to alumina (QAL) > convert to Aluminium (Al Smelter) > cast and roll to shape > ship to Hoogevens (Europe) > alloy in remelt in Europe > cut to size > machine to parts > Ship to USA Boeing and assemble in Plane. This is also a value chain since at each step the intrinsic value of the product has increased.
Sustainable Capability	That which can be consistently maintained over a period of time without imposing undue stress on people.
Sustainable Competitive Advantage	That special capability identified by the company that will enable it to attain a superior position in the market with respect to major competitors. Unfortunately, these are not sustainable for long in a global market.

System	All the resources of the supplier including all people, all processes and all external suppliers/contractors – it a sum of all processes. The system efficiency is the product of the individual process efficiencies. For example, E = 0.9*0.9*0.9*0.9*0.9 for 5 processes at individual efficiencies of 0.9; that is, 90%. The system efficiency is therefore 0.59 = 59%.
System Capability	The measure of variation in the value adding system's response with respect to customer's expectations; this is sustainable between the upper and lower boundaries of variation when all special causes have been eliminated.
System Intent	The process of identifying customers' expectations and interpreting these into a form suitable for use within the extended value adding system.
System Performance	Includes both the absolute level of performance of the goods and services as well as the degree of variation about that level.
Tampering	Changing the variables in a process to try and compensate for special causes of variation. This makes the variation worse.
Tactics	The art of placing or maneuvering forces skillfully in battle.
Team	A group of people who have common goals and who work together in a synergistic way to achieve them.
Time Based Management	To gain competitive advantage by minimising cycle times.
Total Productivity	The ratio of the outputs (goods and services) from the company to the sum of the four basic inputs (labour, material, capital and energy).
TQC	Total Quality Control – organized activities involving everyone in a company, managers and workers, in an integrated effort towards improving performance at every level. This improved performance is directed toward satisfying such cross-functional goals as quality, cost, scheduling, manpower development and new product development. It is assumed that these activities ultimately lead to increased customer satisfaction.

TQM	Total Quality Management is the management approach that achieves continuous incremental improvement in all processes, goods and service through creative involvement of all people.
TQS (The Quality Solution)	A total solution to a strategic business improvement, linking: • Teamwork • Measurements • Processes • Training and Education • Quality Assurance • Continuous Improvement with Strategy and Vision
Trigger Point (T)	The Inventory value at which a signal is generated to produce.
Twenty Six Rules for JIT Use for Large Product Ranges for Short Runs	• **People** 1. Continuously improve the culture 2. Team-up 3. Optimise customer response • **Integration** 4. Supply equals demand 5. 'Pull' for minimum cycle-time 6. Apply to supply chain 7. Minimise variation 8. Shorten the financial cycle 9. Apply *6S System* • **Planning** 10. Demand to bottleneck 11. Even mix for production 12. First in first and prioritise 13. Optimize supply 14. Load-levelling 15. Equal batches at the Economic Production Run (EPR) 16. Optimise sequencing • **Operations** 17. Minimize waste 18. Aim for continuous flow 19. Maximise value-added 20. Link processes

	21. Match processes 22. Minimise hold points 23. Prevention not rework 24. Use Statistical Process Control (SPC) to improve control to Six Sigma 25. Use Single Minute Exchange of Dies (SMED) 26. Use quality systems as part of the business processes
Value added (materials related)	The amount that purchased raw materials and components increase in vale when they have been converted into products.
Value Added Work	That part of an employee's activities that is perceived as adding value (not cost) to the company's goods and services.
Value Chain	See Supply Chain. The only difference is the different degree of focus on supply in terms of delivery on time and cost, and value added (profit or increase in value).
Values	The basis upon which decisions are made and actions taken; Or The types of conduct (personal, group or enterprise) that are seen as acceptable and desirable; Or The things the enterprise stands for and believes in.
Value Stream Map	Flowchart linking operations with data boxes aimed at line-balancing and inventory reduction.
Variable Data	Characteristics that you measure on a numerically graduated scale.
Variable Data Recording Sheet	A simple tool used for collecting and recording variable data.
Variation	Exists throughout the entire value adding system and is the 'enemy' to achieving and sustaining a long-term customer supplier relationship.
Vendor Managed Inventory (VMI)	see Consignment Stock
Velocity	Speed with direction

Vertical Integration	The extent of process span, direction of process boundary expansion and the balance between resulting linked activities.
Visible Management	The technique of providing information and instruction about the elements of a job in a clearly visible manner so that the worker can maximise his productivity.
Vision	Underlying a mission statement is a picture, an image, a vision of a desired state of affairs that inspires action, determines behavior and fuels motivation.
Wholesale	Sale in large quantities especially for the purpose of resale
WIP	Work in Progress; usually the term used to describe the goods that have been booked out from raw materials and have not had all the value added by the manufacturing processes and have not been booked into finished goods. Typically, WIP values for non-JIT processes are 1000 times greater than batch process non-JIT systems.
X-bar (Average) Chart	A graphical technique used to measure whether the process is centered on target or the nominal value.

Bibliography

Akerlof G. A., Shiller R. J. (2009): *Animal Spirits: How Human Psychology Drives the Economy and Why it Matters for Global Capitalism*, Princeton University Press, Princeton, New Jersey, USA.

Allen, Robert (1980): *How to Save The World*, Corgi Book, Transworld, London, England.

Altov H. (1994): *And Suddenly the Inventor Appeared*, Technical Innovation Ctr.

Anthony S. D., Cobban P. (2019): Breaking the barriers to innovation, *Harvard Business Review*, November–December.

Athos A. G., Pacale R. T. (1981): *The Art of Japanese Management*, Penguin Books Limited, Harmondsworth, Middlesex, England.

AiGroup (2019: Australian Manufacturing in 2019, May 2019, page 5.

AiGroup (2019): Australian Manufacturing in 2019, May 2019, page 16.

Australian Small Business & Family Enterprise Ombudsman (2019): *Small Business Counts*, page 41.

Beckman B, Giani A., Carbone J., Koudal P., Salvo J., Barkley J., (2016): Developing the digital manufacturing commons. *Procedia Manufacturing*, volume 5, pages 182–194.

Bendell A., Disney J., Pridmore W. A. (1989): *Taguchi Methods*, IFS Publications, Springer-Verlag, Berlin, Germany.

Benyus J. M. (1997): *Biomimicry, Innovation Inspired by Nature*, Harper-Collins Publishers, Inc., New York, USA.

Bernstein P. L. (1996): *Against the Gods, The Remarkable Story of Risk*, John Wiley & Sons, Inc., Canada and USA.

Berry L. M., Houston J. P. (1993): *Psychology at Work*, WCB Brown and Benchmark, Oxford, England.

Betti F., De Boer E., Giraud Y. (2020): Industry's Fast-Mover Advantage: Enterprise Value from Digital Factories, McKinsey & Company, January.

Blakemore Consulting Website (2011): viewed online 23 April 2011, http://www.blakemore.com.au/; http://www.blakemoresource.com/.

Blakemore J. S. (1979): Galvanizing of Intricately Shaped Products, AU-B 85985/75, Patent Acc 498153.

Blakemore J. S. (1991): Private visit and communication.

Blakemore J. S. (1995): *Quality Habits of Best Business Practice*, MASC Publishing and Prentice-Hall, AIM Competitive Edge Series (1996).

Blakemore J. S. (1998): Future Innovation Strategies, World Innovation and Strategy Conference, August 1998, pages 243–251.

Blakemore J. S. (2001): Maximising Profitability with Short Production Runs, *Technology Business Review*, AGSEI Permission granted 12 December 2007 to the David B. Graff of the United States Air Force Air University, USA, ph 801-230-9397.

Blakemore J. S. (2005): The Creative Innovative Company Program, in Conjunction with the Australian Federal Government's Innovation Access Program.

Blakemore J. S. (2007): The Lean Creative Innovative Company Program in Tasmania, *New Engineer*, March, 2007, vol. 10, no. 1, part of the Creative Innovative Company Program and the Innovation Access Program for the Australian Government.

Blakemore J. S. (1991): The Quality Solution at Precision Valve, Quality Australia, September.

Blakemore J. S. (1998): Technology Creates Business Opportunities, *Technology Business Review*, September.

Bransford J. D., Stein B .S. (1984): *The Ideal Problem Solver*, W. H. Freeman and Company, New York, USA.

Brown J. A. C. (1954): *The Social Psychology of Industry*, Pelican, Penguin Books, Harmondsworth, Middlesex, England.

Capgemini Technology Innovations. https://www.capgemini.com/.

Champy J. (1995): *Reengineering Management*, Harper Business, Harper-Collins Publishers, Inc., New York, USA.

Charney C. (1991): *Time to Market, Reducing Product Lead Time*, Society of Manufacturing Engineers, Dearborn, Michigan, USA.

Cimarosti A. (1997). *The Complete History of Grand Prix Racing*, Aurum Press Limited, London, England.

Clarkson J. (2009): *Top Gear* Assessment by readers for the 42 car manufacturers in the world.

Collaborating to gain a competitive advantage, events, MM, February 2019.

CSIRO Futures (2019): Manufacturing, May.

CSIRO (2018): The last word, To develop, create & grow, L. Marshall, CSIRO, *Manufacturing Monthly*, March, page 42.

Dassault Systems (2020): Cloud-enabled digital transformation of product development, *Lifecycle Insights*, Dassault Systemes, Solidworks, 4 May.

De Bono E. (1967): *New Think*, Avon Books, New York, USA.

De Bono E. (1985): *Six Thinking Hats*, Penguin Group, London, England.

Deloitte Access Economics (2020): Productivity is not an accident: The economics & impact of Victoria's start-up ecosystem, *Deloitte Access Economics*, June.

Deming W. E. (1982): *Out of the Crisis*, Massachusetts Institute of Technology, Centre for Advanced Engineering.

Design Council (2011): A business innovation infrastructure with design inside, *Design for Innovation*, Design Council, page 10.

Egawa M., Yoshino M. (2002): Nissan Motor Co., Ltd., Harvard Business School N9-3030-042, 24 October 2002.

Einstein, A .(1950): *Out of My Later Years*, The Wisdom Library, New York, USA.

Fayol H. (1961): *General and Industrial Management*, Sir Isaac Pitman & Sons, Bath, England, UK.

Feigenbaum A. V. (1986): *Total Quality Control*, McGraw-Hill International Edition, Industrial Engineering Series, New York, USA.

Feltex Initial Public Offering (IPO) (2003) and Investment Statement and Prospectus, First NZ Capital and Forsyth Barr and Feltex Carpets Annual Reports 2004 and 2005.

Forrester J. (1964): *Industrial Dynamics*, Cambridge, MIT Press, Massachusetts, USA.

Fraser J. (2020): Why strategy matters to Industry 4.0 success, *Tech-Clarity*, June.

Global CEO Survey (2020): Industrial manufacturing trends 2020: Succeeding in uncertainty through agility & innovation, *23rd Annual Global CEO Survey: Trend Report*, PWC, June.

Goennemann J. (2018): *Building Resilience in Australian Manufacturing*, Advanced Manufacturing Growth Centre (AMGC).

Goennemann J. (2020): Advanced Manufacturing Growth Centre (AMGC), 5/3/2020.

Goering K., Kelly R., Mellors N. (2018): *Adopting Disruptive Digital Technologies in Making & Delivering*, McKinsey & Company, 2018.

Goldman S. L., Nagel R. N., Preiss K. (1995): *Agile Competitors and Virtual Organisations*, Van Nostrand Reinhold, New York, USA.

Goldman S. L., Nagel R. N., Preiss K. (1996): *Cooperate to Compete*, Van Nostrand Reinhold, New York, USA.

Goleman D. (2006): *Emotional Intelligence*, Bantam Books, New York, USA.

Haden J. (2019). A study of 2.7m start-ups found the ideal age to start a business (& it's much older than you think), *Inc.*, June, https://www.inc.com/jeff-haden/a-study-of-27-million-startups-found-ideal-age-to-start-a-business-and-its-much-older-than-you-think.html.

Harry M. J. (1993): *The Nature of Six Sigma*, Motorola University Press.

Holweg M., Pil F. K. (2004): *The Second Century*, The MIT Press Cambridge, Massachusetts, London, England.

Hughes A. (2008): Australian Business Forum on Innovation, Sydney.

Imai M. (1986): *Kaizen: The Key to Japan's Competitive Success*, Random House Business Division, New York, USA.

Industry 4.0 digitisation of SME infrastructure, www.dematec.com.au/june-11-2019.html, 23 March 2020.

Ishikawa K. (1982): *Guide to Quality Control*, Asian Productivity Organisation, JUSE Press, Tokyo, Japan.

Jones D. T., Roos D., Womack J. P. (1990): *The Machine That Changed the World*, Rawson Associates, Macmillan Publishing Company, Canada.

Juran J. M. (1974): *Juran's Quality Control Handbook*, McGraw-Hill Book Company, New York, USA.

Kaku M. (2005): *Parallel Worlds: The Science of Alternative Universes and our Future in the Cosmos*, Penguin Books, London, England

Karatsu A. (1990): As relayed to me in Japan 1985 at Panasonic.

Kimura R., Reeves M., Whitaker K. (2020): *The New Logic of Competition*, BCG, 15 February.

Liker J. K. (2004): *The Toyota Way: 14 Management Principles from the World's Greatest Manufacturer*, McGraw-Hill, New York, USA.

Macquarie Dictionary (1998): Free enterprise, The Macquarie Library, Macquarie University NSW, Third Edition.

Main L. (2020): The perfect age to become CEO, *Financial Review*, February 24.

Maxton G. P., Wormald J. (2004): *Time for A Model Change*, Cambridge University Press, England, UK.

Mayo E. (1927): *The Hawthorne Effect*, studies at the General Electric Company in Chicago.

Mayo R., Moody P. E., Nelson D. (1998): *Powered by Honda, Developing Excellence in the Global Enterprise*, John Wiley & Sons, Inc., New York, USA. Endorsed by James Womack.

McGregor D. (1987): *The Human Side of Enterprise*, McGraw-Hill Book Company and Penguin Books England, UK.

Montgomery D. C. (1985): *Statistical Quality Control*, John Wiley and Sons Inc., Singapore.

Morita A., Reingold E. M., Shimomura M. (1986): *Made in Japan, Akio Morita and Sony*, William Collins Sons & Co., Glasgow, UK.

Moroney M. J. (1951): *Facts from Figures*, Penguin Books, London, England.

Motorola University Press (1993): *Motorola Quality Briefing, Melbourne Australia, and The Nature of Six Sigma Quality*, Motorola University – training of all Blakemore staff.

Myers R. H., Walpole R. E. (1993): *Probability and Statistics for Engineers and Scientists*, Macmillan Publishing Company, Macmillan Inc, New York, USA.

Noonan W. (2017): Victoria leading the way, *Manufacturing Monthly*, July, page 7.

Ott E. R. (1975): *Process Quality Control*, McGraw-Hill Book Company, New York, USA.

Ouchi W. G. (1981): *Theory Z: Japanese Management Practices*, Addison-Wesley Publishing Company, Inc., Philippines.

Patterson L. (2018): How to successfully bring new products to market, *Industryweek*, 1 September.

Porter M. E. (1990): *The Competitive Advantage of Nations*, The Macmillan Press Limited, London, UK.

Gittins R. (2020): Productivity issue? Let's start @ the bottom, not the top, *Business Age*, 2 March, page 23.

ReVelle J. B. (2002): *Manufacturing Handbook of Best Practices*, The St Lucie Press, Washington DC, USA.

Roberts C., Private communication following our consulting assignment conceptually designing three new production lines at the Sydney plant.

Ross P. J. (1988): *Taguchi Techniques for Quality Engineering*, McGraw-Hill Book Company, New York, USA.

Scientific American (1995): *Key Technologies for the 21st Century*, W. H. Freeman & Col, New York, USA.

Senge P. M. (1990): *The Fifth Discipline,* Century Business, Bantam, Doubleday, Random Century Group, London England.

Shewhart W. A. (1931): *Economic Control of Quality of Manufactured Product,* D. Van Nostrand Company, Inc. New York, USA

Shingo S. (1983): *Shinguru Dandori,* Japan Management Association, Tokyo, Japan.

Siemens Digital Industries (2020): *Deliver Quality, Fast & Informed Designs,* Siemens Digital Industries Software, 5 February.

Smith A. (1776): *An Inquiry into the Nature and Causes of the Wealth of Nations,* Oxford University Press, UK.

Soon F. (1997): Asia Pacific Service and Quality Conference, Singapore.

Stalk Jr. G., Hout T. M. (1990): *Competing Against Time,* The Free Press, Collier, Macmillan Publishers, London, UK.

Taylor F. W. (1911): *Principles of Scientific Management,* Harper New York, USA.

Technical Innovation Centre, Inc., Worcester, Massachusetts, USA.

The Engineering Profession, A Statistical Overview, 14th edition, Engineers Australia, June 2019.

Thomsen S. (2020): A new accelerator, The Melt, is cranking up Australian manufacturing after investing in 5 start-ups, www.startupdaily.net, 21 September 2020.

Wundt W.: University of Leipzig – Wundt initiated the first studies dedicated to the scientific study of human behaviour.

Yoshino M. (2002): *Leading Change,* Australian Institute of Management & Harvard Joint Training Program, Sydney, Australia.

Zimbardo P. (1973): A Pirodellian Prison, *The New York Times Magazine,* 8 April.

Index

For Product Safety Concerns and Information please contact our EU
representative GPSR@taylorandfrancis.com
Taylor & Francis Verlag GmbH, Kaufingerstraße 24, 80331 München, Germany

www.ingramcontent.com/pod-product-compliance
Ingram Content Group UK Ltd.
Pitfield, Milton Keynes, MK11 3LW, UK
UKHW021109180425
457613UK00001B/6